DYNAMICS OF

VisiCalc®

DYNAMICS OF

VisiCalc®

Barry D. Bayer

Joseph J. Sobel

DOW JONES-IRWIN ☐ Homewood, Illinois 60430

The financial template discussed in Chapter 6
is available from the authors on disk format.
For further information contact:

Barry D. Bayer
P.O. Box 1506
Homewood, Illinois 60430

© DOW JONES-IRWIN, 1983

All rights reserved. No part of this publication may be
reproduced, stored in a retrieval system, or transmitted,
in any form or by any means, electronic, mechanical,
photocopying, recording, or otherwise, without the prior
written permission of the publisher.

This publication is designed to provide accurate and
authoritative information in regard to the subject matter
covered. It is sold with the understanding that the
publisher is not engaged in rendering legal, accounting, or
other professional service. If legal advice or other expert
assistance is required, the services of a competent
professional person should be sought.

*From a Declaration of Principles jointly adopted by a Committee
of the American Bar Association and a Committee of Publishers.*

ISBN 0-87094-391-X

Library of Congress Catalog Card No. 82–73621

Printed in the United States of America

1 2 3 4 5 6 7 8 9 0 K 0 9 8 7 6 5 4 3

PREFACE

In the beginning there was the Apple computer, a checkbook-balancing program, and a bunch of games. With 48K of RAM memory, and BASIC in ROM, the Apple II was a powerful computer, but no one except the computer professional or serious computer hobbiest could make it do much. And the typical computer professional was convinced that the Apple was only a toy.

Two Harvard Business School students, Daniel Bricklin and Robert Frankston, knew better; they developed a program that could run on the Apple and which looked like one of their professor's blackboards. Thus was born, for want of a better name, VisiCalc, the VISIble CALCulator. At first no one knew what to do with VisiCalc. But as word of the power of this electronic simulation of an accountant's worksheet spread, VisiCalc and the Apple II computer became the preeminent products in their respective fields, and the infant microcomputer industry leaped into the Fortune 500.

We have come to VisiCalc out of a need to use a computer to manipulate data from our respective professions, but without any interest in becoming computer programmers. VisiCalc has worked for us. We have written this book to help make VisiCalc work for you.

The *Dynamics of VisiCalc* was not designed as a cookbook of VisiCalc applications templates nor a tutorial in VisiCalc's basic command keystrokes. Although we have included several VisiCalc templates which you may enter into your computer, it is our hope that you will use this book to enhance your understanding of how to build your own templates to do exactly what you want, exactly the way you want it.

We have not been able to do this alone. The financial model template presented in Chapter 6 and Appendixes C and D was initially suggested by Allen G. Sneider of Laventhol & Horwath's Boston office. Many of the other examples come from problems presented by our clients. Parts of this book have appeared in different form in *The Apple Orchard, Harvest,* the journal of the Northern Illinois Apple Users Group, and *Desktop Computing* magazine, and we are indebted to the editors and readers of these publications for their comments and encouragement. We must also thank Jerrold H. Bents, Thomas A. Farin, and L. Darryl Mataya for introducing us to the VisEXEC concepts presented in Versacalc 16!, and the people at Software Arts, Inc., and VisiCorp for their assistance.

This book could not have been written without the cooperation of our families. Our wives Susan and Bette Jo put up with the time taken to plan, write, and revise. Our children, David, Elisabeth, Jonathan, Michael, Stephen, and William, reluctantly stopped using our computers long enough so that we could use them to complete our work.

This book must also be dedicated to Messrs. Bricklin, Frankston, Wozniak, and Jobs, without whom all of this would not even have been a dream.

Barry D. Bayer
Joseph J. Sobel

CONTENTS

PART I

Getting Started

Introduction 2

1. If You Don't Have a Computer 5
An Accountant's Worksheet. Replication. Functioning.

PART II

Basic Techniques with VisiCalc

2. Basic Template Design 13
Starting Out: *VisiCalcers Beware. Save Your Work Often! Back Up Your Disks. Back Up Your Program Disk. Hints for the IBM and Apple User.* Planning Your Template: *Do It on Paper. Separate Your Input and Output.* How to Enter a Template: *Windows Make It Easier. Always Use Cell References.* Setting the Global Parameters. Global Formats: *Global Column Widths. Manual Recalculations. Order of Recalculation.* More on Replication. Other Basic Planning Considerations.

3. The Ins and Outs of VisiCalc: Printing, Saving, and DIF 31
Saving and Loading: *Reading a File. Naming Disk Files. Loading a File.* Printing: *Setup Strings. "Printing" to Disk.* Data Interchange Format (DIF): *Saving a DIF File. Tuples and Vectors. C R or RETURN.*

PART III

Advanced Techniques with VisiCalc

4. **Advanced Template Design** 45

   More Helpful Hints: *Using Windows. Saving Parts of a Template. Rounding with VisiCalc. Defining Ranges for Easier Alterations. Forward References and Other Misfortunes.* Beginning with Booleans: *More Boolean Functions. The Quasi Booleans.* Using Overlays. Using DIF: *Rolling with DIF. Consolidating with DIF.* VisEXEC Files: *Rolling with VisEXEC. More on VisEXEC.*

5. **Enhancements: Hardware and Software to Use with VisiCalc** 73

   Software Enhancements. Hardware Enhancements.

6. **Designing an Application** 81

PART IV

VisiCalc—The Advanced Version

7. **New Features** 103

   The Financial Functions. The Arithmetic Functions. Returning Labels with the Lookup Functions. Date Arithmetic.

8. **Attributes** 111

   /AE or /GAE Expression. /AH or /GAH Hide. /AM or /GAM Mode: *Protect and Unprotect. The Other Modes.* Making Your Template User Friendly. /AT Tabs. /AL Labels with Gutters. /AV Values: *Displaying Values.* /AD Default.

9. **Making Life Easier** 117

   Keystroke Memory. Clearing Memory. Help Screens. Variable Column Widths. Multiple Replications and Other Goodies. Page-Print Formatting. To Buy or Not to Buy?

APPENDIXES

A. **Command Reference Guide** 127

B. **Function Reference Guide** 141

C. **The Blank Model Template** 161

D. DocuCalc Template Printout 167

Glossary 179

Index 185

PART I

Getting Started

INTRODUCTION

You are a businessman, a student, or a teacher. Or perhaps you are an accountant, lawyer, physician, financial analyst, or real estate investor. You have files of numbers, historical data, and future projections which you must organize to assist you in making a decision. You would like to be able to apply varying assumptions to your numbers to see what might happen if interest rates go down, birth rates go up, or M2B stays the same.

You know what formulas and logical relationships your numbers have, and you can organize them with pencil and paper. It is very tedious, however, to write everything down and figure your answers with a pocket calculator. And a change in one assumption will require a complete recalculation, which will take about as long as the first one. Then, when you're finished, you must send your handwritten output to a typist and a proofreader before distribution to your colleagues or clients. And next month, you can look forward to performing this tedious process all over again.

Maybe you have a data-processing department with large, mainframe computers, which could take your data, prepare the appropriate programs, process your data, and return reports to you. In six weeks. Or maybe six months. But you need your answers today.

You have read about the new, powerful microcomputers and might even have purchased one. But the prewritten programs you have purchased don't do exactly what you want to do with your data. Of course you could write a program to do the job in BASIC, Pascal, Forth, APL, or FORTRAN, but you are not a computer programmer and don't want to become one.

This book is written for you!

VisiCalc, a program written by Daniel S. Bricklin and Robert M. Frankston and marketed by VisiCorp, is generally considered one of the most, if not *the* most, successful program written for the microprocessor. Large national accounting firms are rumored to have recommended purchase of a micro, just to gain an environment for use of this program. Originally written for the Apple II but now available for other machines—such as the Atari 800, the IBM Personal Computer, the Apple III, the TRS-80, and Hewlett Packard equipment—VisiCalc probably comes closer to being a universally used and accepted program than anything else except Pac-Man. "VisiClones" or "CalcAlikes," such as SuperCalc and MagicCalc, now abound, and a spreadsheet program has appeared for the small but mighty Sinclair ZX-81/Timex 1000 twins. With VisiCalc, or another spreadsheet program, a nonprogrammer can manipulate his or her own data and develop very powerful analytic tools.

In this book we will explain, in detail, the workings of VisiCalc's commands and built-in functions. More important, we will show you how you can plan and organize the information you need to do your work by utilizing VisiCalc to its maximum efficiency. In addition, we will point out some of the lesser known and nondocumented "features" of VisiCalc. Many of the techniques we will demonstrate are usable, not only with VisiCalc, but with all of the spreadsheet programs.

We will not, except as illustration, present specific VisiCalc "templates" or "grids" to perform specific functions. It has been our experience that such "canned" templates usually must be altered to fit the situation, and that mindless entry and alteration of hundreds of VisiCalc cells is usually more difficult (and conducive to error) than thinking the problem through and setting up the template with appropriate replications. Once you really understand how to use VisiCalc, you will be able to cut your development time and tailor your templates to fit your specific needs. Oddly enough, proper design will make your templates easier to revise as your needs change.

Whenever you use VisiCalc, keep in mind that there are two principal keys to it. The first is an understanding of VisiCalc's capabilities and how to use them. But almost more important is an understanding of your own applications. In this book, we will show you how to combine your knowledge of the problems you must solve with your ever-increasing VisiCalc skills to produce exactly the correct template.

Chapter 1 is an introduction to VisiCalc for those who don't have a computer and have never used a spreadsheet program.

Chapter 2 will give you a thorough grounding in how to design a VisiCalc template, while Chapter 3 explains how VisiCalc communicates with the outside world through your disk drives and printer.

Chapter 4 contains expert-level hints and techniques about template design. Chapter 5 reviews hardware and software peripherals which can be used to make your work with VisiCalc even easier and more productive.

In Chapter 6 we take a real business problem: the hurried creation of a business plan for submission to a banker in support of a loan application. You may never have had a similar problem, but we think that you'll be able to apply the design process outlined in Chapter 6 to develop your own planning techniques.

Chapters 7, 8, and 9 discuss the new Advanced Version of VisiCalc, which we find much more powerful and easier to use than the current standard version.

We hope that Appendix A, a comprehensive listing of VisiCalc commands, and Appendix B, a reference guide to VisiCalc's built-in functions, will own a place on your bookshelf as references in addition to serving as useful guides during the reading of this book.

If you own neither computer nor spreadsheet program and are not sure whether VisiCalc could be useful to you, we hope to help you answer that question. Work through this book, concentrating on the template examples and ignoring the specifics that relate to the computer itself. You will, at the very least, come away with a good understanding of what VisiCalc can and cannot do. Then you will be able to decide if a spreadsheet program is for you.

Having noted that this book will be valuable to readers without computers, we should add that it is not intended as a guide for raw beginners with computers. If you own a computer and VisiCalc, we assume that you can turn on your computer, boot (start up) VisiCalc, and format data disks. We also assume that you have at least read through the manual that comes with VisiCalc and that you have your VisiCalc reference card at hand. If you have that minimum of training, we can help you to unlock the dynamics of VisiCalc.

We will often distinguish between a template *user* and a template *designer*. By *designer* we mean the person who enters the formulas and formats into the VisiCalc workspace. By *user*, we mean a person who loads a predesigned VisiCalc template and uses it to manipulate the data that he or she enters. We intend this book to make you a *designer*, or at the very least, an informed template *user*.

In this book, we have used brackets with bold type to indicate special function keys. They are listed below, along with the functions they control.

>**[RETURN]** or **[ENTER]**
>**[ESC]** (escape)
>**[CTRL]** (control)
>**[REPT]** (repeat)
>**[/]** (to start command)
>**[;]** (to change windows)
>**[!]** (to recalculate)
>**[RESET]**

We are not programmers—we are professionals, a lawyer and an accountant. We began by studying our computers' instruction manuals just to get the devices working to begin with. We need our information processed our way, and we have neither the time, money, skill, nor inclination to prepare our own programs or to hire consultants. With VisiCalc, we have been able to get our computers to work for us. In this book we will show you how to use VisiCalc to get your computer to work for you.

CHAPTER 1

If You Don't Have a Computer

AN ACCOUNTANT'S WORKSHEET

Imagine an accountant's worksheet. You know what we mean. It is ruled off into rows and columns, and it is printed on very good paper so that errors can easily be erased. The sheet probably has room for 40 rows and 10 or 12 columns, and it can be used for everything from calculating trial balances to posting batting averages, from scribbling luncheon orders to creating models of international market interactions.

VisiCalc is basically an electronic simulation of that same accountant's worksheet. But VisiCalc has 63 columns lettered A to BK and 254 rows numbered 1 to 254. Each cell is named for its coordinate column and row designation. For example, the cell in the upper left-hand corner of the sheet is called A1; the cell in the upper right-hand corner is BK1; the lower left-hand corner cell is A254; and the cell in the lower right-hand corner is BK254. You can make entries to any cell, just as on your paper worksheet. But if you make a mistake with VisiCalc, you can correct it without an eraser, simply by covering the cell with the cursor and typing in the new data or formula.

Because of memory limitations in most microcomputers, not all rows and all columns may be used at the same time. However, even the smallest of the microcomputers will have available memory for hundreds of cells, and this should be plenty of space for most of the applications that we will discuss in this book.

The VisiCalc user can enter three types of information into any cell: labels, numbers, or formulas. A label is simply the name of something, consisting of normal alphanumeric characters. Labels are useful for heading columns or rows, leaving notes for the user, and putting lines, borders, and the like into report formats. Labels are mostly ignored by VisiCalc when it does its calculations. Typical labels are SALES, PROFITS, TOTAL, ____.

A number is—well, a number. Like 1, 2.3142342, 6.00. Numbers are also digits strung together with numerical operators +, −, * (for multiplication), and / (for division). Numbers are used by VisiCalc when calculating.

Formulas combine numbers, references to other cells, and many built-in commands. A typical formula is "1.1*A2". This formula, when placed in Cell A3, would tell VisiCalc to take whatever value was in Cell A2, multiply it by 1.1, and place the answer into A3. As a result, A3 would always be 10 percent larger than A2.

If A4 were specified as "1.1*A3", A5 as "1.1*A4", and A6 as "1.1*A5", the number in A6 could represent the number in A2 compounded over four periods of time. For example, "1000" (dollars) placed into A2 would yield "1464.10" if compounded at 10 percent simple interest for four years. If you have a hand calculator with exponents, this is the same as the formula

$$((1000*(1.1))\wedge 4)$$

where "∧4" means "to the fourth power". We can change this example slightly, so that the compounding factor "1.1" would instead be contained in cell A1; it could thus be used as a variable. Our formula may now refer to Cell A1, and Cell A6 would be shown as "(A5*A1)". Figure 1.1 shows a VisiCalc Screen displaying the example we have just discussed.

Cell A2 contains the value 1000. The formulas in Cells A3, A4, A5, and A6 are quite similar; they each reference the compounding value in Cell A1, and they each multiply this compounding value by the value in the preceeding cell in order to compound the earlier value. If you think of the templates that you have created on paper, you will realize that cells are often related in similar ways. When such relationships occur, we can replicate the formula in a cell to a series of other cells, without being required to enter the formula directly into each cell.

After entering the formula "(A1*A2)" into Cell A3, the VisiCalc user can enter the command "/R" to begin a sequence which will replicate the formula in Cell A3 into Cells A4, A5, and A6—or, in typical VisiCalc terminology, from the "Source Range A3...A3" into the "Target Range A4...A6".

REPLICATION

The operation of the REPLICATE command is difficult to describe, but the replication concept is so important to VisiCalc that we should conduct a preliminary discussion of the subject here.

The REPLICATE command, initiated by "/R", permits you to copy the contents of one or more cells to another group of one or more cells. The cells that are copied are known as the *source range*, and the cells that are copied *to* are the *target range*. The source range may consist of a single cell or a series of adjacent

1: If You Don't Have a Computer

FIGURE 1.1: AN ANNOTATED VISICALC SCREEN

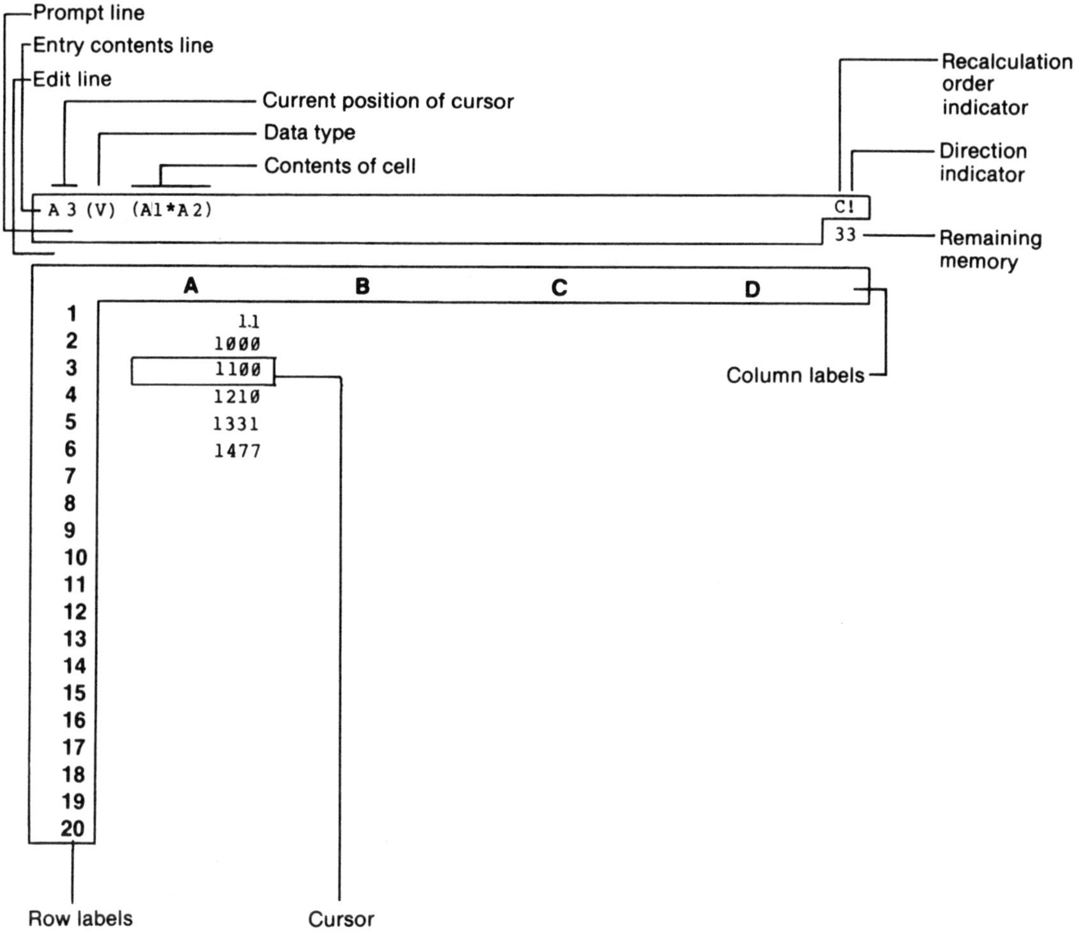

```
┌─Prompt line
│ ┌─Entry contents line
│ │ ┌─Edit line                                                    ┌─Recalculation
│ │ │         ┌─Current position of cursor                         │  order indicator
│ │ │         │    ┌─Data type                                     │
│ │ │         │    │      ┌─Contents of cell                       │   ┌─Direction indicator
│ │ │         │    │      │                                    C1  │   │
│ │ └─ A 3   (V)   (A1*A2)                                     33 ─┴───┴─Remaining memory
```

	A	B	C	D
1	1.1			
2	1000			
3	1100			
4	1210			
5	1331			
6	1477			
7				

Column labels (A B C D) — Row labels (1–20) — Cursor on A3

cells in the same row or column. The target range may consist of a single cell, a series of adjacent cells in the same row or column, or even a rectangular area. We'll save the more complicated types of replications for Chapter 2 and Appendix A, but replicating the example discussed above is rather simple.

Place the cursor on Cell A3, and type "/R". VisiCalc's edit line will read "A3" and the prompt line will now read

REPLICATE:SOURCE RANGE OR RETURN

Press [**RETURN**], and the "CARRIAGE RETURN" key, [**ENTER**], or whatever your computer calls it, and the prompt line will now read

REPLICATE:TARGET RANGE

and the edit line will read

A3 ... A3:

This means that the source range has been entered and begins with Cell A3; it also ends with Cell A3. (In other words, the source range is the Cell A3.) Type in "A4.A6" and hit another **[RETURN]**. The prompt line will now say

REPLICATE: N=NO CHANGE, R=RELATIVE

The edit line will now read

A3:A4...A6:A1

and A1 will be highlighted in inverse video or some other fashion.

The A4...A6 means that the target range has been identified, beginning with Cell A4, and ending with Cell A6. The "A1" begins the formula in Cell A3.

After identifying the source and target ranges, VisiCalc will highlight each formula reference in the source range and ask whether the reference should be replicated "relative" or "no change." If "no change," the target cell will reference exactly the same cell as the source cell; if "relative," the target cell will contain a reference with the same location relationship to the target cell as the source cell's reference to the source cell. Thus if Cell D4 contained a reference to Cell C3, the target cell E4 should contain a relative reference to Cell D3 (one up, one to the left).

As we have seen above, the A2 reference should always be to one cell above the current cell, and is therefore relative. The A1 reference, on the other hand, is always to A1, and should therefore be "no change."

As soon as you type the "N" for the A1 reference, "*A2" is added on the edit line and the highlighting will move from A1 to A2, requesting, in effect, "R" or "N" for the A2 reference. Hit "N", and you will see VisiCalc calculate each cell in the target range, making separate entry into each target cell unnecessary. This is not terribly impressive if you are using only four cells. But what if you wanted a year-by-year analysis for each of the next 20 years? Or month-by-month, for that matter? This ability to avoid the entry of large groups of cells is one of the most important features of VisiCalc. "REPLICATE," as previously stated, is a *very* important command.

Of course, the real power of VisiCalc comes now, when you can ask "What if . . . we start with $8765.32?" Or "What if . . . we compound at 12 percent per year?" Try putting "8765.32" into Cell A2, and "1.12" into Cell A1 for the answer to these and other fascinating questions.

FUNCTIONING

We now understand how a VisiCalc spreadsheet (we will be calling it a grid, worksheet, or template) is set up, how to replicate, and the value of using cell references. But before we really get into exploitation of the dynamics of VisiCalc, we should really talk about VisiCalc's built-in functions.

A function is a "black box" which accepts one or more inputs and returns an output. As long as we know what input to give to a function and what output to expect, we don't know or care how it does what it does. Using VisiCalc, we can do a number of things—such as finding the net present value of a range of cash flow, determining the sine of an angle, or computing the mean average of a series of grades—merely by specifying the name of the function and the input to be given to the function. VisiCalc uses the character "@" to signify the beginning of the name of many functions. Appendix A contains a complete summary of the VisiCalc built-in functions, but let's take a look at one function here to see how it works.

The built-in function "@SUM" tells VisiCalc to add the values located in a series of specified cells, which we will hereafter call a list, or, if the cells are adjacent to each other, a range of cells. A range may be specified by entering its beginning cell and ending cell, either by typing in the cells' coordinate names (A1 or B17), or by "pointing" to each cell by moving the VisiCalc cursor to each of the two cells. Ranges may be either horizontal—that is, all in one row—or vertical—all in one column. All ranges are lists, but as each range consists of adjacent cells, and this is not required by a list, not every list constitutes a range.

If we wanted to find the total of the five amounts in Range A3...A6, the statement

@SUM(A3...A6) or @SUM(A3,A4,A5,A6)

when placed in Cell A8, would be equivalent to the formula

A8 = A3+A4+A5+A6

Of course, you could also type "+A3 + A4 + A5 + A6" into Cell A8, but "@SUM" is so much easier. If you wanted to add the values in Cells A1, A2, A3, etc., all the way up to A50, placing the formula "@SUM(A1...A50)" into Cell A100 would save even more time.

Now that we know how to use "REPLICATE" and "@SUM", we understand the beginnings of what VisiCalc can do. We are now ready to begin working with VisiCalc.

PART II

Basic Techniques with VisiCalc

CHAPTER 2

Basic Template Design

STARTING OUT

A detailed description of how to get VisiCalc working with your particular computer is not presented here. If you have never used your computer, we suggest that you study the operating manuals and learn how to turn the machine on, how to "boot" a disk, how to save and load programs and data, and how to use your printer. Spending an hour or two on such preliminaries is well worth it if you have not previously had the pleasure.

If you are generally familiar with the basic operation of your computer, you can probably get VisiCalc going without difficulty. The introductory section of the VisiCalc Manual will take you by the hand in exploring your computer's mechanics if you do have any problems.

Once you can get VisiCalc up and running you should work through the tutorial in the VisiCalc Manual. When you're finished, turn off your computer and continue reading this book.

VisiCalcers Beware

You will be spending lots of time working with VisiCalc, and you will be generating template files which will become quite valuable to you. The warnings below are applicable to normal computer operations, with or without VisiCalc. Please heed them. Disasters have a habit of occurring at the most inopportune times.

Save Your Work Often!

We suggest that you save the current state of your VisiCalc work every few minutes, whether designing a template or entering data. This will minimize time wasted in reconstructing a template if a malfunction should cause you to lose the contents of your computer's memory. Of course these things won't happen to you—but we have experienced power failures, heat buildup, and static electricity discharge, and we have been very unhappy when required to reconstruct a template that has taken hours to complete.

The worst type of computer malfunction is, of course, the operator who unthinkingly clears memory (by typing ''/CY''—Clear, Yes) or even turns off the computer prior to saving the file. Strange things happen in computers used at 3 AM. Whatever the problem, the time taken to save the current state of your template every 10 or 15 minutes will pay dividends when you least expect them.

Saving the current file is particularly easy to do, as VisiCalc permits you to review the names of the files on your disk directory by successive applications of the ''→'' (right arrow) key when VisiCalc prompts for a filename after entry of the ''/SS'' (Storage, Save) command. When the appropriate filename appears on the prompt line, you may record over that file by pressing **[RETURN]**. Respond with a ''Y'' to VisiCalc's question about replacing the old file. We suggest that you should retain at least one copy of your old file every few saves; add a trailing character or number to the name on the edit line to denote that this is an updated version. (If ''EXAMPLE'' is your old filename, your revised file could be ''EXAMPLE.1''.) This will create a new file and leave the original intact. Retaining the old file will ensure continuity in case your computer should choose the middle of a disk save as an appropriate time to quit. When your disk is full, you can delete all but the last couple of versions of your file, using the ''/SD'' (Storage, Delete) command.

Back Up Your Disks

Back up your disks containing templates and data. Do it as a matter of unvarying routine, just like brushing your teeth. Keep your backups in a safe place, preferably other than the one where you keep your working copies. Damage by earthquake, fire, theft, strong electromagnetic fields (which could ''erase'' a disk doing no noticeable physical damage), coffee, dogs, or children do occur. A backup in another location could become a lifesaver.

By the way, in the event of casualty loss, many property damage insurance policies will reimburse you for the cost of blank disks but not for the cost of replacing data encoded on them. Read your insurance policy, or ask your insurance agent about your coverage. But backups are still the best insurance.

We recommend using one of two different backup procedures. The first is to make a copy of your disk after clearing VisiCalc at the end of each session.

VisiCalc templates and data are stored in standard text files, which can be duplicated using your computer's disk-copy programs. The other method is to save each file twice, once on your original data disk and immediately thereafter on a backup data disk. This is most easily accomplished if you have two disk drives. Whichever method you decide on, we suggest that you follow it as a matter of routine. If you don't do it automatically, the chances are you won't have a backup when you really need it.

All of this is, no doubt, quite a bother. Until you lose a file you can't afford to lose. We promise you that it will come in handy one day.

Back Up Your Program Disk

Make or purchase a backup copy of the VisiCalc program disk itself. This is a small price to pay should your original fail at a crucial time. Many versions of VisiCalc are sold with a so-called copy protection scheme, making normal disk-copy programs unusable. However, special copy programs are available to make VisiCalc backups. An archive copy of VisiCalc is a necessity. Consult with your attorney if you have any questions as to the status of archive copies of legally obtained programs under the federal copyright laws, or under any license agreements that you may have entered into. Purchase a backup copy from VisiCorp if you must, but do get one. Then put it away in a safe place.

Hints for the IBM and Apple User

If you have an Apple II DOS 3.3 version of VisiCalc, check the version number which appears on the edit line when the program is first booted. (The number disappears as soon as a key is pressed. To get the version number back, enter "/V".) Version 193B0 contains a significant bug in the DIF save routine, which could destroy your ability to access files from that particular disk.[1] If you have version 193BO you should obtain the latest updated version, 208B0 or 218B0 for the //e, from VisiCorp as soon as possible. In the meantime, don't try to save more than one or two DIF or print-to-disk files on one disk.

If you use an IBM PC, you should make sure that you have placed your current version of DOS on the VisiCalc disk. One of the nice things about VisiCalc is that it outputs files to disk in a standard format that may be read by other programs. If you forget to upgrade your VisiCalc when you upgrade the DOS of the other programs, you diminish this utility.

---

[1]This bug can cause the Volume Table Of Contents (VTOC) and/or some of the directory sectors to be overwritten or destroyed. DOS uses the VTOC and the directory to locate files on the diskette, and the destruction of one or more of these sectors could render your files unusable unless you have a working knowledge of DOS and you are able to repair the damaged disk.

If you are still using an old version of VisiCalc (the 13-sector version on the Apple II, or the original, unenhanced version on the TRS-80 Model I), you should seriously consider upgrading to the more powerful version. This features such enhancements as IF/THEN/ELSE logic and Data Interchange format (DIF). The Apple II DOS 3.3 version also gives you more room for data on your disks.

PLANNING YOUR TEMPLATE

Now that we have finished the preliminaries, let's get started with VisiCalc itself.

Planning a VisiCalc template is easier than writing a computer program. But the statement that a nonprogrammer can effectively use VisiCalc, although true, may be just slightly misleading. The nonprogrammer can make effective use of VisiCalc, but only by applying a group of commonsense rules which are (or should be) common practice among programmers as well. VisiCalc is not (exactly) a programming language, but the clearer the logic of the user's advance plan, the better the template is likely to work.

The following techniques may seem to require extra time to follow, but they will save you much more time in the long run.

Do It On Paper

Plan your template on paper before turning on your computer. Yes, it may have said something like that somewhere in the VisiCalc documentation, but it really does work. And as always, *Avoid the temptation to just start entering data without thinking.*

Use a specially printed VisiCalc planning sheet like CalcPad™,[2] or a sheet of columnar paper, or just a piece of paper. But at least sketch out what you want to do before you turn on the computer. The things to keep in mind, at this point, are what inputs you will be starting with, the reports that will be your finished product, and the formulas that will be required to transform the former into the latter.

Determine the appropriate order of recalculation and column width as part of the design (see pages 25–26). Although VisiCalc defaults to column order of recalculation and a 9-character-per-column width, it does not mean that these default values should be used just because they are there.

Work from the upper left of the worksheet to the lower right, staying within the rectangle formed by your work as much as possible. This will conserve memory and generally result in a more efficient worksheet. Once you begin to

---

[2]CalcPad is a trademark of PadWare, Limited.

enter the template into your computer, you may find that your version of VisiCalc works faster if you make a dummy entry to what you estimate will be the lower right of the sheet before you begin entering your labels, formulas, and numbers. This is caused by the way that VisiCalc manages the computer's memory; it will not affect the actual template in any way.

FIGURE 2.1

	A	B	C	D	E
1		Q 1	Q 2	Q 3	Q 4
2	SALES	15000	17250	19838	22813
3	COST	6750	7763	8927	10266
4		------	------	------	------
5	GROSS	8250	9488	10911	12547

Imagine that VisiCalc is working only with the cells included in a rectangle defined by cell A1 in the upper left-hand corner and the active cell furthest to the lower right of the template in the opposite corner. In Figure 2.1, entry of data in Cell C8 will cause VisiCalc to pause while it reallocates memory to consider an additional group of cells. However, if a dummy entry is made into Cell G9, all of the cells in Columns F and G and also in Rows 6 through 9 will immediately become available, without a reallocation pause. We understand that this feature may not present a problem in future versions of VisiCalc. But if you have the problem in your current version, you now know how to solve it.

Separate Your Input and Output

The typical worksheet should contain a *data* area, a *calculation* area, and a *report* area. Any two or all three of these types of areas can be combined, particularly in a small template. But a complex template calls for well-defined areas. Data to be entered by the user, and tables and variables to be used in calculations should be in the data area. This area should usually be towards the upper left of the sheet, where it can be accessed by VisiCalc before subsequent cells are recalculated. This technique helps to eliminate circular and triangular references. Intermediate calculations which will not be displayed in the final report should also be kept in the the calculation section. The report area will consist of the actual format to be used in a formal presentation. Alternatively, it may merely be a section near the bottom of the worksheet used to summarize the resulting calculations in a form suitable for presentation purposes.

Figure 2.2 is a simple template which will forecast sales, cost of goods sold, and gross profits for five periods. (The period under study could be a month, a year, or a day. It doesn't matter which, as long as we make sure that the units we are using are designed for the period we are forecasting.)

FIGURE 2.2

	A	B	C	D	E	F
1	**					
2	**					
3	PERIOD	1	2	3	4	5
4		--------	--------	--------	--------	--------
5	SALES	15000	15750	16538	17364	18233
6	COST GC	7500	7875	8269	8682	8205
7		-----	-----	-----	-----	-----
8		7500	7875	8269	8682	10028

The following items are entered into the listed cells:

Cell	Contents
B5	15000
B6	.45 * B5
B8	(B5 − B6)
C5	1.05 * B5
C6	.45 * C5
C8	(C5 − C6)
D5	1.05 * C5
D6	.45 * D5
D8	(D5 − D6)
E5	1.05 * D5
E6	.45 * E5
E8	(E5 − E6)

This template does a fine job, as long as we wish to assume that sales always grow at a fixed percent per period and, that cost of goods sold is always equal to 45 percent of sales. If we wish to begin the series with sales of $10,000 for the first period, instead of $15,000, we need only change B5 from 15000 to 10000. But if we wish to change the growth rate to 7 percent, or cost of goods sold to 41 percent, we will be required to change Cells C5, D5, E5, and F5, and each of the cells in Row 6. Figure 2.3 shows the same template divided into a data area and report area.

FIGURE 2.3

	A	B	C	D	E	F
1	***					
2	********DATA AREA********************************					
3	BEG SALES	15000				
4	GROWTH RT	.05				
5	CGS RT	.45				
6						
7	***					
8	********REPORT AREA******************************					
9	PERIOD	1	2	3	4	5
10		--------	--------	--------	--------	--------
11	SALES	15000	15750	16538	17364	18233
12	COST GS	6750	7088	7442	7814	8205
13		------	------	------	------	------
14	GROSS PRF	8250	8663	9096	9550	10028

The cell contents of the first two lines of the report now look like this:

Cells	Contents
B11	(B3)
B12	(B5 * B11)
C11	(B11 * (1 + B4))
C12	(B5 * C11)
D11	(C11 * (1 + B4))
D12	(B5 * D11)
E11	(D11 * (1 − B4))
E12	(B5 * E11)
F11	(E11 * (1 + B4))
F12	(B5 * F11)

With this framework, we can change initial sales levels by changing B3, the periodic growth rate by changing B4, and the percentage cost of goods sold by changing B5. It is this "what if" ability that gives VisiCalc much of its appeal. But you can't "what if" easily if you don't design your template properly. Division of your design into data areas and report areas will help.

HOW TO ENTER A TEMPLATE

Although *Dynamics of VisiCalc* is not designed as a spreadsheet "cookbook," we will use sample templates to demonstrate our work throughout the book. While we will not tell you exactly how to enter each template into your computer, we will often show the contents of key cells, with some indication of how to replicate a formula if replication is needed. Obviously, the listings of cells in Figures 2.2 and 2.3 are a bit bulky. Instead, we will use a format where each line will start with a ">" (GoTo) symbol, which indicates the cell in which the entry must be made. For example the entry in cell C22 would be shown as:

>C11:(B4*(1+B4))

Replications will show the beginning cell, the "/R" replication command, indications of the range to be covered, and a sequence of Rs and Ns, which show whether each referenced cell, in sequence, should be replicated RELATIVE or NO CHANGE. The colons (:) interspersed within the line indicate that **[RETURN]** should be pressed. The C11 cell, for example, should be replicated as follows:

>C11:/R:D11.F11:RN

Remember, we will not show labels, or places where mere numbers are entered, as we are concerned only with cells containing formulas.

Windows Make It Easier

It is often convenient to separate the VisiCalc screen into windows using the "/W" command, with the data area occupying the first window, and the report area the second. Decide whether you want the screen to be split from top to bottom (vertical windowing, done with the "/WV" command) or from left to right (horizontal windowing, the "/WH" command). Move the cursor to one of the 20 rows of data on the screen, issue the "/WH" command, and the row that the cursor was on becomes the break between the windows. The cursor can be moved between the two windows by pressing the **[;]** key.

Setting up the break using vertical windowing is a bit more difficult, and it may be necessary to adjust the column widths until you get the break exactly where you want it. One method, which is not recommended or supported by VisiCorp or Software Arts, but which may work with your version of VisiCalc, is to enter the command "/XVn" where n is an integer from 6 to 34. The vertical window will then be set up at n spaces from the left side of the screen. (It may be necessary to readjust your column widths after you're finished with this.) This works on the Apple II versions of VisiCalc. It may not work on others, but we can guarantee that it will not break your computer to try it.

Always Use Cell References

We have previously discussed the principal of referring to values located in cells in a "data" area, rather than placing numbers directly in a report area. Always have your formulas use references to the cells containing variables rather than entering the numbers directly into the formulas.

2: Basic Template Design

In Figure 2.3, if B11 is January sales, (15000) and C11 February sales, (January sales at a five percent increase), the contents of the cells should not look like

>B11:(15000)
>C11:(B11*1.05)

Using such an approach, if you wish to change the beginning sales amount or the growth rate, you will be required to dig into the template and change formulas. The cells should look like this instead:

>B3:15000
>B4:.05
>B11:(B3)
>C11:(B11*(1+B4))

Now you can change any of the variables by making a single entry in a single cell. Of course, cells adjacent to B4 would include the label "ANNUAL RATE OF INFLATION" and those adjacent to B3 would be labeled "SALES — FIRST PERIOD" or something similar.

These single-entry "variables" give you the ability to play "what if" games with your worksheet by allowing you to change the variables or assumptions conveniently.

Note also that the growth rate could be expressed as a whole-number percentage, which might be easier to enter than a decimal fraction. The formula in C11 would then take care of this by dividing by 100, to convert the percentage to a decimal. All the data-entry variables should be in units convenient for the user. Let the calculation areas in VisiCalc convert liters to gallons, percents to decimal fractions, or whatever. Do not require the template user to do the conversion work. In a more complex worksheet, these conversions could be done in an intermediate calculation area. For example if B4 were expressed as a whole number, B6 could contain the formula "(B4/100)", and B11 would then reference B6 directly. You may wish to include, as part of your formula at B11, an algorithm to round the resulting calculation, so that all totals will "foot" properly (see pages 46-47).

As another example, consider Figure 2.4 where annual interest rates entered as percentages are converted, not only to decimal fractions, but to a monthly figure. Although the template extends only to seven monthly payments, it could obviously be extended to calculate the payments for many additional months.

Enter interest rates in Cell C7. Cell C13 could convert that rate to a decimal fraction for use in other functions, with the entry

>C13:(C7/100)

If the C7 rate is annual, but the formula requiring the interest rate calculates monthly figures, the intermediate formula could also convert to a monthly rate using the formula:

>C13:(C7/1200)

FIGURE 2.4

	A	B	C	D	E
1	**				
2	*** DATA INPUT AREA ***********************				
3	BUYER :				
4	SELLER :				
5	PROPERTY:				
6	LOAN AMOUNT	$	70000		
7	INTEREST RATE:		11		
8	PAYMENTS PER YEAR:		12		
9	TERM (IN YEARS) :		30		
10					
11	***CALCULATED DATA ********				
12	PERIODIC INTEREST				
13	RATE		.0091667		
14	NUMBER OF PAYMENTS		360		
15	PERIODIC PAYMENT :		666.63		
16	ANNUAL PAYMENTS :		7999.56		
17	********REPORT AREA****************				
18			MONTHLY PAYMENTS		
19		BEGIN	--------------		ENDING
20	PERIOD	BALANCE	INTEREST	PRIN'PL	BALANCE
21	--------	--------	--------	--------	--------
22	1	70000.00	641.67	24.96	69975.04
23	2	69975.04	641.44	25.19	69949.84
24	3	69949.84	641.21	25.42	69924.42
25	4	69924.42	640.97	25.66	69898.77
26	5	69898.77	640.74	25.89	69872.87
27	6	69872.87	640.50	26.13	69846.75
28	7	69846.75	640.26	26.37	69820.38

>C13: (C7 / C8)
>C14: (C8 * C9)
>C15: $-((((((C13) + 1) \wedge (C14)) \wedge -1) - 1)/(C13) \wedge -1) * C6$
>C16: (C15 * C8)
>B22: (C6)
>C22: (C13 * B21)
>C22: /R: C23.C28: NR
>D22: (C15 − C22)
>D22: /R:D22.D28: NR
>E22: (B22 − D22)
>E22: /R: E23.E28: RR
>B23: (E22)
>B23: /R: B24.B28: R

Another example which is not entirely obvious concerns calculation of the yield of depositing $2,000 per year for 30 years into an Individual Retirement Account, with the ever-increasing sum invested at a defined interest rate (see Figure 2.5). The "year" in Column C10 merely picks up C5 with the formula +C5. The other years in Column C add 1 to the cell above, with the "/R" command doing the rest of the work:

>C11:1+C10

FIGURE 2.5

	B	C	D	E	F
2		I.R.A.	CALCULATIONS		
3	GROWTH RT		14 % PER YEAR		
4	MAR TX RT		40 %		
5	START YR	1982		CUR AGE 34	
6	AGE 66	2014		ANN DEPOS 2000	
7					
8	$$				
9	YEAR #		YEAR	IRA	NON-IRA	SAVINGS
10		1	1982	132430	15853	116576
11		2	1983	116166	14625	101542
12		3	1984	101900	13491	88409
13		4	1985	89386	12446	76940
14		5	1986	78409	11482	66927
15		6	1987	68780	10592	58188
52		43	2024	0	0	0
53		44	2025	0	0	0
54		45	2026	0	0	0
55					
56				1062070	189097	872973
57				IRA	NON IRA	SAVINGS

We calculated the retirement value of the first year's $2,000 by the formula

$$>D10: @IF(C10<C6,((E6)*((1+(C3/100))^{\wedge}(C6-C10))),0)$$

where E6 is equal to $2,000, C3 to 14, and C6 to the year in which the IRA contributor reaches the age of 66. The next year's deposit's retirement value (D11) was calculated the same way, substituting the year in C11 for the year in C10.

Now it is a fact of computer life that calculations using exponents (the "^30" factor) are very time consuming. (Try using exponents with a hand calculator and you'll note the same phenomenon.) In fact, Figure 2.5 originally took 67 seconds to recalculate on an Apple II, and a reported 56 seconds on the IBM PC. It may be clear to you (although it was not originally clear to us) that

$$((1.14)^{\wedge}29) = ((1.14)^{\wedge}30)/(1.14)$$

As all other references in both D10 and D11 are identical, D11 could better be expressed as:

$$>D11: @IF(C11<C6,(D10/(1+(C3/100))),0)$$

and replicated down the line. Note that the intermediate figure (C3/100) is used a number of times, it could also be calculated once and referenced.

The same approach was used with Column E, which calculated the value of aftertax deposit and earnings using the marginal tax rate entered into C4. E10 looked something like this:

$$>E10: @IF(C10<C6,(E6*((100-C4)/100))*$$
$$((1+(((100-C4)/100)*(C3/100)))^{\wedge}(C6-C10)),0)$$

and this formula was replicated down Column E. After revision, E11 was simply

>E11:@IF(C11<C6,(E10)/(1+(((100−C4)/100)*(C3/100))),0)

Once again, such repetitive terms as "100−C4" could have been calculated once and then referenced.

These revisions saved a considerable amount of time when recalculating. In fact, the time that was required to recalculate the template as it was first written was reduced to eight seconds on both the Apple and the IBM PC. While this example is more dramatic than most, eliminating repetitive calculations should always be a desired goal.

The design of the rest of this particular template will be discussed in Chapter 4, with the introduction of the "@IF" function.

SETTING THE GLOBAL PARAMETERS

Now that we have done some preliminary planning on paper, we are ready to turn on the computer and begin the real-time construction of our worksheet.

Four global commands—"/GF","/GC","/GO", and "/GR"—should be entered immediately, as soon as VisiCalc is loaded and ready for use. These commands are each initiated with "/G", and they govern the way the template will look and operate.

GLOBAL FORMATS

VisiCalc has a series of display format options. The default option is "General", and it can be set by a "/GFG" (that is, a global, format, general) command. The general format left justifies labels, right justifies numbers, and it displays numbers to as many significant decimal places to the right of the decimal point as may be permitted by the column width. Trailing 0's to the right of the decimal are dropped. Thus 3.100 would be displayed as 3.1.

Set the global format, if it is to be other than "General", using the "/GF" command followed by the appropriate format symbol, "D", "F", "L", "R", "$" or "*". "L" left justifies; "R" right justifies; "$" rounds the display (but to the value used by VisiCalc internally in its calculations) to two decimal places, including trailing 0's; and "*" formats the cell in VisiCalc's so-called graphics mode. Careful thought should be given to using a global format which will minimize the necessity for entering local formats in individual cells. This will conserve memory which would be used by the local format commands contained within the cells, and also simplify data entry and template design.

For example, assume that you want a column of numbers displayed to at least five decimal places, but most other columns are to be displayed as dollars and cents. In such an example, the global format should be set to "/GF$", and the cells in the column to be displayed with more than two decimal places should be set individually, by replication of course, to "/FG". Also, note that year headings (1983, 1984, and the like), should always be shown as Integers. "1983.00" does not look very professional.

Global Column Widths

The global column width should be set with the "/GC" command. The column width should be set to at least one space greater than the maximum number of digits to be displayed, to allow for the "+" or "−" sign. Also remember to include an additional space for a decimal point, if applicable. Allow enough characters for the largest total or numeric display you expect to have on the worksheet. Remember that a cell containing totals may require more digits than the data being totaled.

But column width can also be too large, as anyone knows who has ever attempted to print out a report requiring 9 columns of information with a column width of 9 characters per column, on a printer with a maximum of 80 characters per line. Recent generations of dot matrix printers can switch to a 132-character line on 8-inch-wide paper, which is, perhaps, at least a partial answer to the problem. Sometimes the only way to get all the information printed is to revise the entire layout of your template or to print out in several passes. You must also consider your printing requirements in terms of the number of columns you can print on a page at the desired column widths and the appearance of your sheet if data became too cramped. Proper planning before you start, including consideration of matters such as those discussed above, will save you a great deal of time later.

Manual Recalculations

"Recalculation" should always be set to the manual mode with the "/GRM" command. When the program is in the automatic recalculation mode, the worksheet is recalculated each time that the **[RETURN]** key is pressed. You do not require recalculation each time you enter a number or formula. Manual recalculation will avoid annoying pauses each time you enter data into a cell. You can always force a recalculation by pressing the [!] key, even when you are in the manual mode. The "/GRA" (global, recalculate automatic) command will change the template back to automatic recalculation mode, if necessary.

Order of Recalculation

Each time the [!] key is pressed, or, in the automatic recalculation mode, every time the **[RETURN]** or **[ENTER]** key is pressed, VisiCalc reviews each active cell in the template, updating the value of each cell reference, recalculating through each formula, and updating each cell to display its recalculated value. The order of recalculation is shown as an "R" or "C" in the upper right corner of the screen, above the "remaining memory" indicator. VisiCalc always begins a recalculation in the upper left corner in cell A1. But recalculation can proceed either in column order, down column A, (recalculating first A2, then A3 and eventually A254 before proceeding to B1), or in row order, across Row 1 (recalculating first Cell B1, C1, D1 and eventually to BK1 before proceeding to A2). VisiCalc, when recalculating, will always use currently entered numbers wherever they are on the template. But if a formula references a cell containing formulas which have not yet been recalculated in the current recalculation sequence, VisiCalc will use the old (then current) value, rather than the value that it will have at the end of the sequence, which has not yet been calculated. Thus an inappropriately chosen order of recalculation can result in inaccurate output from an otherwise satisfactory template.

Figure 2.4, a typical interest amortization schedule, provides a good example of problems with order of recalculation. The interest column is calculated by multiplying the monthly interest rate by the beginning balance for the period in question, listed in the beginning balance column. The interest figure, in turn, is subtracted from the periodic payment cell, to calculate the portion of the payment which is allocable to principal. That amount, in turn, is subtracted from the beginning balance to determine the ending balance. And the ending balance on one line becomes the beginning balance for the next.

Develop such a template, or walk through Figure 2.4 by hand using a column order of recalculation. You'll find that it just doesn't work, as the application simply requires a row order of recalculation. If you use column order in such a worksheet, you will find that you need numerous recalculations to obtain the proper results when calculating multiple repayment periods. The order to be used will depend upon your particular application. If you notice that it takes several recalculations to obtain the proper results, the order of recalculation may need to be changed. But you can usually determine the proper order for your template when sketching it out *before* you turn on your computer.

The order of recalculation can be set by the "/GOR" (global, order, row) or the "/GOC" (global, order, column) command, as appropriate. "/GOC" is the VisiCalc default, but, as shown above, it is not necessarily correct for a particular template. Your template plan, made before you turned on the computer, should tell you which order is required. Just make sure that, if part of your template requires column order, another part doesn't require row order.

MORE ON REPLICATION

In Chapter 1 we showed how to replicate from a source range consisting of a single cell to a target range consisting of multiple cells. The complete lineup of possibilities are as follows:

Type	Source (from)	Target (to)
1	Single cell	Single cell
2	Single cell	Adjacent cells in row or column
3	Adjacent cells in row	Adjacent cells in row
4	Adjacent cells in row	Adjacent rows
5	Adjacent cells in column	Adjacent cells in column
6	Adjacent cells in column	Adjacent columns

If this outline seems confusing, we suggest that you sit down and try to work out the various possibilities on a piece of paper. The time you spend in working on the replication command will be worth it.

When the source range (where you are copying *from*) is defined as a single cell, the target range (where you are copying *to*) may be either a single cell or a range of cells (Type 1 or Type 2 in the chart). If the source range is defined as a multiple-cell range, the target range in Type 3 and Type 5 is simply specified as a single cell which begins the target range. If the source range is five cells long, VisiCalc knows that the target range must also be five cells long, and requires only the beginning point. VisiCalc will supply the end of the range—any ending that you supply will only confuse things.

Type 4 and Type 6 replications define target ranges that are rectangular areas. But instead of the upper-left/lower-right type of definition so common in VisiCalc, to obtain a replication of rows (Type 4), the target range is defined by the first cell of the row beginning the target range and the first cell of the row ending the target range. The first cell of the column beginning the target range and the first cell of the column ending the target range define the target range for a replication of columns (Type 6). Remember, once you have defined the beginning of the target range, VisiCalc completes the definition to copy all of the cells in the source range.

As you consider these various combinations, remember that replication always requires the following steps:

1. Identify the source range.
2. Identify the target range.
3. State whether each cell reference in the source range should be replicated "R" for "Relative," or "N" for "No Change."

If you keep these three steps in mind, you can't go too far wrong.

Let's take an in-depth look at an example of one of the more complex types of replications in order to illustrate the point. In Figure 2.6, Cells A6 through A8 contain the formulas:

>A6:(A2*A3)
>A7:(A2*A4)
>A8:(A2*A5)

Here are the keystrokes necessary to accomplish the replication of Cells A6 to A8 into Columns B through D.

Keystroke	Explanation
>A6	GoTo Cell A6.
/R	Begin the replicate command starting with Cell A6 (the edit line now shows the beginning of the source range followed by three dots).
.	Informs VisiCalc that you want to specify the balance of the source range and you are about to indicate the end of the range.
A8	Specifies the end of the source range.
[RETURN]	Informs VisiCalc that you have completed the entry of the source range.
B6	Indicates that you want the replication to start in Cell B6.
.	Informs VisiCalc that you want to specify a target range and you are about to indicate the end of the range.
D6	Indicates that you want to replicate the column of entries in A6 through A8 into Columns B through D.
[RETURN]	Informs VisiCalc that you have completed the command and to proceed with the replication. (Since Cells A6 through A8 contain formulas, VisiCalc's prompt line now reads "REPLICATE: N NO CHANGE R RELATIVE"; the formula contained in the first source cell, A6, is shown on the edit line; and the first cell reference in the formula is highlighted.)
R	Informs VisiCalc that you want the first cell reference to be replicated "relative" so that the cell reference will always bear the same positional relationship within each of the target cells.
N	Informs VisiCalc that you want the second cell reference to be replicated "no change" so that the same cell will be referenced in the formula in each of the target cells.

The formulas in each of the succeeding cells, A7 and A8, are then placed on the prompt line so that you may indicate the nature of the cell reference as "relative" or "no change." After "R" or "N" has been specified for the last cell reference in each formula, the formula is placed in each target cell and those cells are calculated, based upon the data in the balance of the template.

The target range we specified was B6 through D6. Notice that we have not indicated anywhere that we wanted Cells A6 through A8 to be placed in Cells B6 through B8, C6 through C8, and D6 through D8. VisiCalc is smart enough to understand our desires in this type of replication. If we specified the target range as B6, the upper left of the rectangle containing the target range, and D8, the lower right of the target range, we would actually confuse VisiCalc and it would beep at us.

As always, we suggest that you write down your replications on your planning sheet before you enter them into the computer. A little bit of advanced planning saves a lot of redoing.

FIGURE 2.6

	A	B	C	D
1	456	456	456	456
2	10000	11000	12000	13000
3	.10			
4	.12			
5	.14			
6	1000	1100	1200	1300
7	1200	1320	1440	1560
8	1400	1540	1680	1820

OTHER BASIC PLANNING CONSIDERATIONS

Set your local formats for individual cells as you enter a number or formula, and certainly do it before you replicate a formula. You cannot easily replicate just a local format into a cell after you have entered data into it.[3] Once again, thinking before typing will pay huge dividends in time saved and aggravation eliminated.

VisiCalc automatically displays the column letters and row numbers of the cells displayed on the VisiCalc screen; they appear across the top and down the left side respectively. Printouts of the worksheet, however, usually lack this convenience.[4]

Planning and debugging of complex worksheets may be simplified by printing these "borders" on the printout. To include the borders, place the VisiCalc cursor on Cell A1. First insert a row ("/IR") moving all data in the template down one row, and then insert a column ("/IC"), moving everything one column to the right.

>A1:/IR
>A1:/IC

Each formula and cell reference on the template automatically adjusts to the new locations of the referenced cell. Now type an "A" in cell B1, a "B" in C1, and so on, for each of the columns you wish to print. You may wish to "center" the letter identifying the column by typing a quotation mark (") and several spaces before typing the identification letter, or you may even wish to fill the entire space by making the identification letter a repeating label, using the "/-" command. Although the letter *A* is now in column B, column B contains what was designed to be column A. A bit confusing, but we promise it will work out all right. Now GoTo Cell A2, and enter the number 1. The formula "1 + A2" goes into Cell A3, and A3 may then be replicated as far down as necessary for the printout.

---

[3] But see pages 56–59 about overlays.
[4] The screen print function on the IBM PC will print the entire displayed screen, including the identification, "borders," but a standard printout, using VisiCalc's "/P" commands, will not have these borders.

>A2:1
>A3:1 + A2
>A3:/R:A4.A50:R

will extend the numbering down to A50 (which should contain the number 49). If you are using a ''/GF$'' or ''/GF*'' format, you may wish to set a local integer format in Cell A3 before replication.

After the template (or the portion of the template you are interested in reviewing) is printed, go back to Cell A1 and delete one column and one row.

>A1:/DC
>A1:/DR

The template will adjust back to its original state, moving everything back to the left and to the top, automatically deleting the borders, updating all formulas, and enabling you to work on the template once more.

If you find this technique useful, you may wish to design an otherwise blank template which has only borders for rows and columns. This template may then be ''overlayed'' upon your working template (after it is been moved down and to the right, of course), saving a considerable amount of time.

CHAPTER 3

The Ins and Outs of VisiCalc: Printing, Saving, and DIF*

The most convenient data-manipulation program would be useless without a method of communicating the results of the manipulations. When your VisiCalc template is complete, you will want to save the template to disk or other offline storage medium. Some versions of VisiCalc permit saving of files to cassette tape, but we do not recommend this particular storage medium if disks are available. Once saved, a template may be used again and again. You may wish to print all or part of the template so that it may be used to communicate the results of your work with others. Finally, you may need to take the same data that have been entered in the template, or that may be the result of calculations made by the template, and use them in another template or in other programs. You may even wish to use certain data in other parts of the same template. VisiCalc makes provisions for accomplishing each of these tasks.

VisiCalc's printing function is initiated with a "/P" command, which directs the printing of the labels and calculated values in a user-defined rectangular area of the template. The printed data look very much like those shown on the VisiCalc screen display, reflecting the calculated values of your formulas. Thus the entry

$$>A10: (A1+A2)$$

will be printed or displayed as the arithmetic sum of the values in Cells A1 and A2. The printing function may also be directed to a disk rather than to the printer,

---

*DIF is a registered trademark of Software Arts, Inc.

which will enable the user to incorporate a VisiCalc report into standard text files such as those generated by many word processors. We have used this capability extensively while writing this book.

Saving and loading functions are initiated with a "/S" command. "/SS" directs the "saving" of the actual contents of each cell of the entire VisiCalc template. Although each cell's format, if any, is saved, the label, value or formula is saved just as you typed it rather than as it appears on the screen. Thus the entry

$$>A10:(A1+A2)$$

will be saved to disk in just that format. "/SL" initiates the load function of VisiCalc and permits a template which has previously been saved to disk with the "/SS" command to be recalled into the computer for reuse.

The DIF (Data Interchange Format) I/O is initiated by the "/S#" command. "/S#S" saves and "/S#L" loads a rectangular area of the VisiCalc template. Thus one can save the values resulting from the formulas contained in each cell within the defined area. With a DIF save, the calculation results and/or the alphanumeric data, but not the formulas, can be used by other programs, or even reused by VisiCalc itself. In this chapter we will discuss each of these modes of communication from and to VisiCalc.

SAVING AND LOADING

"/SS" (Storage, Save) is the basic VisiCalc "save" and will store the current stage of active VisiCalc memory to a disk file, so that it may be read back into VisiCalc with a "/SL" (Storage, Load) command. The file saved is a standard computer ASCII textfile, which can be read without the use of VisiCalc, and which is probably compatible with your computer's word processor program if the latter uses standard textfiles. Throughout this book, we will refer to such files as "/SS" or logic files.

Reading a File

Consider Figure 3.1, which compares this year's results with last year's results and calculates the percentage difference between the two, according to the formula

((THIS YEAR) − (LAST YEAR)) / (LAST YEAR)

Now compare Figure 3.1 with Figure 3.2, which is a listing of the same template in exactly the form of an "/SS" save to your printer.

A review of Figure 3.2 reveals much about VisiCalc. The file is saved and loaded, starting with the bottom row on the right and ending with the top row on

FIGURE 3.1

	A	B	C	D
1		THIS YEAR	LAST YEAR	% DIFF
2	INCOME	134567	121345	.1089620504
3	EXPENSE	124561	101212	.2306939889
4		--------	--------	--------
5	PROFIT	10006	20133	-.503005017

the left. Because of the way VisiCalc manages its computer memory (see pages 16–17), it is more efficient for formulas to be read back into the computer starting at the lower right of the template, and the "/SS" file is saved just that way. Also, each entry is preceded with a ">CELL LOCATION:" symbol, which tells VisiCalc where the following entry belongs. Cell A5, and others, have an entry which is preceded by quotation marks. This signifies that the entry is a label rather than a value. This label identifier is added by VisiCalc where the user inputs an alpha label without a preceding " inputted by the template designer. On the other hand, the parentheses that precede the value entries have been supplied by the template authors. D5 could have been written as

>D5: +D2−D3

instead. But the "+" or "(" is required to tell VisiCalc that "D" is really the start of a value entry. The "+D2−D3" obviously denotes cell references, while the contents of C3, for example, is the number 101212.

The listing ends with five lines which begin with a [/]. The first four lines tell VisiCalc which global parameters have been set. Figure 3.2 shows one window, column order of recalculation, automatic recalculation mode, and a column width of 12. The very last line supplies information as to the location of the window in the VisiCalc workspace, and the position of the VisiCalc cell cursor.

FIGURE 3.2

```
>D5:(B5-C5)/C5
>C5:(C2-C3)
>B5:(B2-B3)
>A5:"PROFIT
>D4:"   --------
>C4:"   --------
>B4:"   --------
>D3:(B3-C3)/C3
>C3:101212
>B3:124561
>A3:"EXPENSE
>D2:(B2-C2)/C2
>C2:121345
>B2:134567
>A2:"INCOME
>D1:"    % DIFF
>C1:"LAST YEAR
>B1:"THIS YEAR
/W1
/GOC
/GRA
/GC12
/X!/X>A1:>A1:
```

FIGURE 3.3

	A	B	C	D
1		THIS YEAR	LAST YEAR	% DIFF
2	INCOME	134567	121345	10.90
3	EXPENSE	124561	101212	23.07
4		--------	--------	--------
5	PROFIT	10006	20133	-50.30

These last five lines are the settings that were maintained when the file was saved with the "/SS" command.

Local formats have not been used in this template. However, a "/F$" format could have been used in column D, combined with a multiplication by 100 to convert the decimal fraction to percent. Figure 3.3 above shows the neater appearance of column D that would result.

The altered column D formula listing would appear as follows:

>D5:/F$((B5−C5)/C5*100)
>D3:/F$((B3−C3)/C3*100)
>D2:/F$((B2−C2)/C2*100)

The local format "/F$" precedes the entries in the cells.

It should not be necessary to say so, but whenever you are saving anything—and this includes printing to disk, as you will see below—have a blank initialized (formatted) disk on hand. If you encounter a "disk full" error, you can resave your file onto this empty disk, immediately. It may be possible to format a disk within VisiCalc, but it is also possible to lose the train of creative thought that you had when you first wanted to save the file. Obviously, this is one of many hints in this book born out of the bitter experience of one or both of the authors.

A VisiCalc template can be saved with data, as shown in Figure 3.1, or without data, saving only the template formulas, labels and global parameters (see Figure 3.4). Note in Figure 3.4 that we have indicated the cells in which numbers should be entered with a "<<   >>" entry. These markers are used only to catch the eye of the user and add nothing to the template calculations. Once the template is complete, save it ("/SS") without data to be entered by the user. This will provide the user with a blank template which may be taken as a starting point for each new project requiring a similar solution. Such an approach will help avoid problems created when the user misses a portion of the required data entry and/or leaves inapplicable numbers from a previous model in the current template.

FIGURE 3.4

	A	B	C	D
		THIS YEAR	LAST YEAR	% DIFF
1	INCOME	<< >>	<< >>	ERROR
2	EXPENSE	<< >>	<< >>	ERROR
3		--------	--------	--------
4	PROFIT	0	0	ERROR

There are two ways that you can study a template in the "/SS" format that is shown in this chapter. The first is to read a saved file into your word processor or text editor. If the word processor uses a format that is standard for your computer, the chances are great that the "/SS" file is compatible. Remember, this will give you a printout similar to that shown in Figure 3.2 and will not provide a text file in report format. However, this is a useful way to study and review a template. The second way is to use VisiCalc to print the listing directly to the printer. With the Apple II, the command is "/SS" followed by ",S" and the printer slot number, rather than the file name. Apple ///s use ".Printer" as the destination, and the IBM PC will use ".LPT1" or some such designation. TRS-80s will require a "/SP" command. Check your VisiCalc manual for the command for your particular computer.

Naming Disk Files

The easiest way to update an existing disk file is to record over it. After entering "/SS," keep hitting the right arrow key until the name of the file you wish to save appears on the edit line. When you reach the desired filename, press **[RETURN]**. You will then be prompted to press "Y" to confirm that you do want to replace the existing file. A "Y" will finish the saving process; anything else will cancel the command and clear the prompt line. If you wish to save the latest version of your template without eliminating the old one, "right arrow" through the catalog again until you get to the correct filename, append a ".1" to the file name, and then press **[RETURN]**. The result will be a new file saved under a slightly different filename, version ".1" obviously being the latter. This method of naming disk files reduces the possibility of typing errors. It may also eliminate the confusion of having several files with similar names and not knowing which is the latest version. After using the right arrow key to cursor through the catalog to the latest version, you may use the **[ESC]** (escape) key to erase the trailing version number and then add a new version number. Some computers will add a suffix to your filename such as "/VC" (many of the TRS-80 machines) or ".VC" (the IBM PC). This suffix is not visible from VisiCalc, and it is of no importance unless you wish to use the file outside of VisiCalc—with your word processor, for example. If your computer adds a suffix, your VisiCalc will not be able to read the file unless the suffix is part of the name.

Loading a File

Loading ("/SL") is the reverse of saving and will enable VisiCalc to use the same template that you have previously saved. "/SL" does *not* clear the VisiCalc workspace, and will generally combine the template on disk with whatever already exists in the computer, giving precedence to the new file in case of conflict. The moral of this little story is to always clear the computer's memory (with the "/CY" command) before loading in a new template if you intend to get exactly the same template that you saved. As discussed on pages 56–59, you may use this feature of VisiCalc to overlay two or more existing templates in order to arrive at a modified result.

PRINTING

"/P" initiates a sequence which will print a rectangular portion of the template in the same format as shown on the screen. This printout will show labels, to the extent of the global column width which has been set; values contained within cells; and values which result from the formulas contained within cells. The formulas themselves are not printed, nor are windows or titles recognized.

To print a template, place the cursor on the cell in the upper left corner of the rectangular area you wish to print, and type "/P," to initiate the sequence. You will usually print to your printer and should therefore type **[RETURN]**.

Setup Strings

VisiCalc will usually find your printer interface and ask for

SETUP STRINGS PRINT: LOWER RIGHT, "SETUP , −, &

This message is a bit cryptic but translates to English without too much trouble. Going from right to left, the "&" key may be pressed if you wish VisiCalc to insert an extra linefeed at the end of each line. You may want to do this if your printer or interface card do not generate a linefeed automatically or if you simply prefer to double space between lines. If your printer or interface normally generates a linefeed each time you type **[RETURN]**, enter a "−", unless you want to double space your report. Your printer or your interface card can usually be adjusted to give the linefeed/carriage return configuration that you require, but VisiCalc is smart enough to do it in software instead of requiring you to fiddle with printer switches. VisiCalc will "remember" the "&" and "−" you enter as long as the program continues to run, so you are usually required to enter these symbols only with the first print run of a particular VisiCalc session.

'"SETUP' is the function that permits you to tell your "smart" printer or interface card what to do. First take a look at your hardware manuals and find out what you must tell your printer to get the results that you want. Some Centronics printers, for example, normally print only 40 columns wide, and you must enter

Control − I 80 N or **Control − I 132 N**

to get 80-column or 132-column printing, respectively. Many printers will print in a compressed type, generally 16.5 characters per inch, after a code, such as a "Control-O" is sent to the printer. Compressed type permits the user to generate 132 character lines on 8 inch wide paper. Some equipment may require a character preceded by the "ESCAPE" code, a carriage return, or a hexadecimal (base 16) number. VisiCalc can do any of these, and more.

To enter setup string mode, hit the quotation mark (") key and start entering your special codes. VisiCalc does not recognize control codes if you hold down the **[CTRL]** (control) key while pressing another key. Therefore, you must use a "/\C" to precede a control character (without the quotation marks of course), "/\E" to generate an escape, "/\H" to output the two characters following the "H" as a hexadecimal number, "/\R" for a carriage return, "/\L" for a line-feed, and "/\/\" for a single "/\". These codes may be strung together. For example, "/\CI/\R/\EA/\H3A" translates as

> Control-I
> [RETURN]
> ESCAPE A
> 3A (base 16).

Your printer or interface card may or may not remember a print string from printing to printing within a session, so experiment. But now you can do wide printouts, italics, boldface, or whatever else your printer is capable of. All from within VisiCalc.

As a final step in the "/P" sequence, type in the coordinate location of the lower right cell of the rectangular area to be printed, or move the cursor to that location. Assuming that your printer is "on" and properly connected, hitting **[RETURN]** will start the printer going, and a printout of the rectangle that you have defined should result. VisiCalc never checks if the printer is working. If your printer is not turned on, or not online, VisiCalc may appear to lock up. This printer condition is not always obvious, and the condition may look like a computer malfunction. Turning the printer on or placing it online should cure the problem.

"Printing" to Disk

Entering an "F" or "D" after the "/P" ("/PF" or "/PD") will cause exactly the same report to be "printed" onto your disk instead, under the filename you specify. Cells, order, column width, will each be the same as for a paper printout. Each line is stored on disk as a separate string, or record, terminated by a carriage return (Control-M). The file will be saved as a standard textfile and will differ from the "/SS" save-to-disk in that the file will not contain the "GoTo" (>) commands with each cell's values or labels, and it will print values rather than saving the formulas. This will allow further manipulation of the file with any program (such as a word processor) which can use a standard textfile.

File naming can proceed just as with "/SS" files. However, some computers will add a ".PRF" or "/PRF" as a suffix to the file name. As with the ".VC" of the "/SS" files, the ".PRF" suffix is of importance only if you are outside of VisiCalc. If your computer does not automatically add a ".PRF" designation, you might want to do so yourself to be able to distinguish between the type of files on a disk.

DATA INTERCHANGE FORMAT (DIF)

One of the more interesting developments to appear in the second stage of VisiCalc was the introduction of Data Interchange Format, or DIF. DIF is intended to act as a software "interface" to exchange data between VisiCalc and other programs, or even between two non-VisiCalc programs. With DIF, for example, data may be sent from VisiCalc to VisiPlot/VisiTrend, and then used to create graphic representations of the data.

"Software Arts, Technical Note (SATN) No. 18," distributed with some versions of the VisiCalc Manual, was our first introduction to DIF. SATN 18 went into long, technical explanations directed toward experienced programmers and involving vectors, tuples, headers, and data, incomprehensible to all but the well-schooled programmer or systems analyst. This situation was not aided by an article appearing in *BYTE* magazine in November, 1981, written by Candace E. Kalish and Malinda F. Mayer of Software Arts, Inc. Although the article was well written, it was not very informative to the layperson. Once again, however, the article contained information valuable to the programmer wishing to use DIF.

Many nontechnical people recoiled from the technical explanations. They thought it would be handy to place VisiCalc-developed information into data bases and programs for graphing and analysis, and to take data from these same sources and manipulate them in VisiCalc. But VisiCalc users hoped that programmers would read the technical information data provided by Software Arts, then develop programs utilizing it. They put aside any hope of being able to use DIF themselves.

Well yes, DIF is complex! But DIF is also very useful in manipulation of data by VisiCalc, to move data between different templates and between different sections of the same template. Using DIF in this manner is simple. Although a technical explanation is not required in order to use DIF in a strictly VisiCalc environment, the balance of this section may help the reader to understand how DIF works and thereby better understand its capabilities and related applications. However, a discussion of how to interface a DIF file with a program in BASIC is beyond the scope of this book. Readers with a consuming technical curiosity about the internal workings of DIF should consult SATN No. 18 and the *BYTE* article.

Saving a DIF File

When VisiCalc saves a rectangular portion of the template as a DIF file, it first converts all of the formulas and referenced values in the saved portion of the file into fixed numeric values. Thus a formula like @LOOKUP(A1,B17...B33) will be evaluated to "765.32", "ERROR" or some other value, and this value, rather than the underlying formula, will be saved to disk. The process is similar to a mass application of the "#" function to all of the formulas in the DIF-fed area, combined with a DIF save.

Tuples and Vectors

VisiCalc thinks of both values and labels as being organized into vectors or tuples rather than rows and columns. But don't get put off by these strange sounding names that must have come from some abstruse scientific discipline. Tuples and vectors are like rows and columns but are relocatable, both as to absolute location and as to vertical and horizontal orientation. Each tuple has an entry (although possibly an entry with a zero value) corresponding to each vector. All of the vector entries comprising a single tuple are placed together. Think of tuples and vectors as X and Y coordinates or rows and columns on a VisiCalc template.

In case the preceding paragraph is not perfectly clear, let's try an example. The data in a typical DIF file might look like Figure 3.5.

It is possible to refer to a piece of data as being in the first tuple and the third vector, just as it is possible to think of a datum in the 18th column and the 50th row—e.g., cell R50.

Rows are always horizontal, and columns are vertical, but DIF-format tuples may be either horizontal or vertical. However, if a tuple is vertical, the vectors are, of necessity, horizontal, and vice versa. Tuples can be placed anywhere in the VisiCalc workspace, although always in the same relationship relative to their corresponding vectors. Thus, values that had been sitting in columns A, B, and C, rows 1 through 10, may be transferred to columns X, Y, and Z, rows 25 through 34, or even to columns X through AG, rows 1, 2, and 3.

FIGURE 3.5

Beginning of first tuple:
Vector A data
Vector B data
Vector C data

Beginning of second tuple:
Vector A data
Vector B data
Vector C data

and so on . . .

C R or RETURN

As part of a DIF save command, VisiCalc requests the user to specify the save in C (for column) or R (for row) order, or just with a **[RETURN]**. When **[RETURN]** is pressed, without specifying row or column order, DIF thinks of tuples as corresponding to rows, and the vectors as corresponding to columns. The same is true for a DIF save in R (for row) order. When C for column is specified, however, tuples become vertical and vectors horizontal. Figure 3.6 shows an example.

Figure 3.6 is a simple template, with both labels (the words "ROW" and "COLUMN,") and numbers. The following sequence of commands:

>B2:/S#S *filename* **[RETURN]** E12 **[RETURN][RETURN]**

will save the template in DIF format, with the rows becoming tuples, and the columns vectors. The beginning data would look something like Figure 3.7, where "BOT" means "beginning of tuple."

FIGURE 3.6

	B	C	D	E
2		COLUMN1	COLUMN2	COLUMN3
3	ROW1	1	2	3
4	ROW2	2	3	4
5	ROW3	3	4	5
6	ROW4	4	5	6
7	ROW5	5	6	7
8	ROW6	6	7	8
9	ROW7	7	8	9
10	ROW8	8	9	10
11	ROW9	9	10	11
12	ROW10	10	11	12

When the DIF file is loaded ("/S#L") with the [RETURN] answer to the "C R RETURN" prompt, the data will be entered into the grid in exactly the same way, tuples across and, necessarily, vectors down.

If we were to DIF save Figure 3.6 in a C (for column) format, however, the DIF file would look a bit different, because VisiCalc would have treated the tuples as being vertical instead of horizontal. Thus the results of a save would look like Figure 3.8.

Notice that in our example, C format results in fewer, longer tuples, and more, shorter vectors than the R, or "RETURN" format. This factor may be of some interest if disk space is at a premium, as the more tuples in a file, the more BOTs will be present, which may result in a somewhat larger disk file.

If we were to reload our DIF saved example, as saved in column format, but reload it in row format, VisiCalc would look at the first tuple and display it across a number of columns, in one row, so that the template would look like Figure 3.9. This results in a 90-degree rotation of the template. This feature is very useful if you are taking information from a template that is organized vertically and placing it into a template with a horizontal orientation. But, as should

3: The Ins and Outs of VisiCalc: Printing, Saving, and DIF

FIGURE 3.7

BOT
""""
COLUMN1
COLUMN2
COLUMN3

BOT
ROW1
1
2
3

BOT
ROW2
2
3
4

BOT

and so on . . .

be obvious by now, a DIF-saved file will come out looking the same as it went in, if you load it in the same row or column order in which you saved it.

We suggest that all DIF saves be in the default "RETURN" format. Then, if you wish to change the format (rotate the file 90 degrees), reload it in C format. That's not quite the intent of Software Arts, but it makes a lot of sense to us. It is a good idea to designate files saved with the DIF option with a filename containing a suffix such as ".DIF", since this file cannot be reloaded with the normal "/SS" command. If you should try to "/SS" a DIF file your computer may beep at you and "EOD" may appear in the cell cursor.

Remember, DIF converts all formulas into the then-calculated values resulting from the formulas. In effect, this "pounds" each DIF-saved cell, thus making the values in those cells impervious to new recalculations. This is extremely useful for transmitting data from one template to another—for example, in "rolling" last month's total into this month's results, or to consolidate the results of separate templates for divisions of a corporation into a template for the entire company. Examples of how this is done are included in Chapter 4.

FIGURE 3.8

BOT
" "
ROW1
ROW2
ROW3
ROW4
ROW5
ROW6
ROW7
ROW8
ROW9
ROW10

BOT
COLUMN1
1
2
3
4
5
6
7
8
9
10

BOT

and so on . . .

FIGURE 3.9

		A	B	C	D	E	F	G	H	I	J
		ROW1	ROW2	ROW3	ROW4	ROW5	ROW6	ROW7	ROW8	ROW9	ROW10
1	COLUMN1	1	2	3	4	5	6	7	8	9	10
2	COLUMN2	2	3	4	5	6	7	8	9	10	11
3	COLUMN3	3	4	5	6	7	8	9	10	11	12

PART III

Advanced Techniques with VisiCalc

CHAPTER 4

Advanced Template Design

MORE HELPFUL HINTS

You've become familiar with the basic VisiCalc commands and built-in functions. You have learned to plan your work before you turn on the computer, and replications are second nature to you. And you know how to communicate from and to your VisiCalc screen. We'll begin Chapter 4 with some additional hints to help you in template design, and then continue with a discussion of Booleans, when to use DIF, and automatic VisiCalc using VisEXEC commands.

Using Windows

Horizontal and vertical windows, synchronized or unsynchronized, are often used to see different parts of the template for reporting or "what iffing" purposes. But windows may also be used to simplify the design of a template. It often happens that one cell will reference another cell in another area of the template. If you have planned your template on paper, it is easy to type in the referenced cell coordinates. If you are not sure of the location of the referenced cell, however, it is often easier to "point" to the cell with the cursor, a procedure explained in the VisiCalc Manual. If the cell in which you are making the entry is far from the cell you wish to reference, it can take quite a while to get to it by pointing with the cursor. If you are pointing to a number of cells in the same area, the windowing function ("/WH" for horizontal windows, or "/WV" for vertical windows) can help. Set your windows so that the cell in which you are entering data is in one window, and the cell to be referenced is in the other.

When entering a formula, you can "point" to the coordinate locations in the other window by using the [;] key to move between windows. You may then move the cursor within that window to the proper location. When you enter the next operand in the formula or hit [RETURN], the cursor will return to the originating window at the cell where the formula is being entered.

This use of the VisiCalc windows is for design purposes only. Eliminate the two windows with the "/W1" command prior to saving the template.

Saving Parts of a Template

VisiCalc has no direct way of saving the formulas and labels from part of a worksheet. If you have a large worksheet and you want to save a block of labels and formulas for use in another template, you can blank out the cells that you don't need (using the "/B" command) and save the cells that you do want. Blanking out a lot of cells can take quite a bit of time, but a blank cell can be replicated, effectively erasing the unwanted cells on a mass basis. With replication you can blank hundreds or thousands of cells using only a few keystrokes.

First replicate a blank cell into a range of cells, to get a blank range. The first cell you replicate must not contain any formatting commands, such as "/F$", unless you actually want those formats at the replicated locations. The remaining portion of the worksheet containing the labels, data, and/or formulas you want to copy may now be saved using the "/SS" command. When reloaded to a blank worksheet, this template will load in at the same cell coordinates from which it was saved. (See the discussion of overlays below.) If you must change locations of the partial template, you can do so by moving rows or columns with the "/M" command, or by inserting or deleting rows and columns with the "/IR", "/IC", "/DR", or "/DC" commands. Inserting and deleting manually can be a lengthy process, but it is possible to automate it with VisEXEC commands (see page 63). Another way to save just a portion of a template is to read the entire file into your VisiCalc-compatible word processor and then erase the rows and columns that you don't want. Once this process is completed, you can save the file with the word processor and then read it back into VisiCalc.

Rounding with VisiCalc

According to the VisiCalc Manual, VisiCalc "retains and rounds to 11 (and sometimes 12) decimal places" within each cell location but may display fewer characters on the screen depending upon local and global formats, etc. However, VisiCalc commands such as "/FI" or "/F$" round numbers only for display purposes and do not round the results of formulas retained in the cell for computation purposes. For example, note Figure 4.1, where column B has been treated with the local integer format ("/FI"), leading to the quite misleading conclusion that $1+1+1=4$. If you wish to be certain that your additions appear to be accu-

FIGURE 4.1

	A	B
1	1.3	1
2	1.3	1
3	1.3	1
4	----	----
5	3.9	4

rate as printed, you must round within the cell formula, rather than using formatting commands.

If you require that amounts be rounded to dollars and cents, etc., for both display and future computation purposes, use the formula in the VisiCalc Manual:

(@INT((*expression*)*100 + .5))/100

Your formula would be inserted into the above rounding formula in place of *expression*. If you need to round to, or display in, some other level of precision, you may adjust the formula accordingly. Three decimal places will require multiplying and dividing by 1,000, one decimal place by 10. The formula

(@INT((123.789) + .5)

without any dividing or multiplying, returns the number 124, rounded to the nearest integer.

Unfortunately, the rounding formula given above, although taken from the VisiCalc Manual, works only if *expression* is nonnegative. Enter

>B1:@INT(A1 * 100 + .5)/100

and experiment entering various values in Cell A1. When 99.999 is placed into A1, B1 correctly shows the answer to be 100. When −99.999 is entered into A1, however, B1 will result in −99.99. An examination of the workings of the @INT function shows why this occurs. @INT(*expression*) tosses away the decimal fractional portion of *expression*. This differs from the INT function in most variations of the BASIC programming language, which returns the next-smallest Integer. Thus, as BASIC INT(−17.31) returns −18, while VisiCalc's INT(−17.31) returns −17.

With the first formula, VisiCalc takes the 99.999 in A1, multiplies it by 100 to result in 9,999.9, and adds .5 to get the sum of 10,000.4. The @INT function returns the value of 10,000, and division by 100 results in a value of 100.00, interpreted by VisiCalc (in general format) to be 100.

Working with −99.999, we get the following stages:

Multiply by 100	−9,999.9
Add .5	−9,999.4
Apply the @INT function	−9,999
Divide by 100	−99.99

The solution, of course, is to *subtract* .5 (or add −.5). In the negative example, −9,999.9 becomes −10,000.4, and the final result is, as expected, −100. The appropriate formula, if a negative number is possible, is

(@INT((*expression*)*100 + @IF(*expression* < 0, −.5, .5)))/100.

The @IF expression works like a switch, inserting a −.5 if *expression* is negative, and .5 in any other case.

You may sometimes wish to round a number to hundreds or thousands (for financial reports, for example). The same formula, with the division and multiplication operators switched around, can be used.

(@INT(123789/1000 + .5) * 1000)

will return the number 124,000.

To finish off rounding, one sometimes wishes to "round" a number to a figure that is other than a power of 10. The current federal tax laws, for example, require that taxpayers use a tax table rather than a tax rate schedule if taxable income is less than $50,000. If one wishes to design a template to convert taxable income to the correct tax, one must simulate the Internal Revenue Service's table structure, which, for incomes exceeding $3,000 deals only with $50 brackets, apparently calculating the tax due in any part of the bracket as the tax due on the midpoint of the bracket. Thus, the tax due on $15,651 and the tax due on $15,699 are each equal to the tax due on $15,675. The trick is to convert taxable income to the bottom of its bracket, to add $25 to the answer, and, using "@LOOKUP", to calculate the tax on the "rounded" number.

(@INT(income/50) * 50) + 25)

You will note that the formula is essentially the same rounding formula used above. For incomes less than $3,000, the IRS requires $25 brackets. Replacing the 50s with 25s, and the 25 with 12.5 achieves the desired result.

Defining Ranges for Easier Alterations

When adding a range of boxes in the same column using the "@SUM" command, or whenever you define a range within a single column, include within your formula the "underlines" under the column heading and after the last figure in the range. In Figure 4.2, the "@TOTAL" figure in Cell C10 should use the formula

>C10:@SUM(C2...C9)

even though the numbers you wish to add are really located in C3 through C8.

Cells C1 and C9, being labels, will be evaluated as zeros and will not affect the totals. If you have to add George's sales, you need only insert a row where appropriate (using the "/IR" command), and need not worry about adjustment of formulas, as the "@SUM" formula will automatically adjust to the expanded

FIGURE 4.2

	B	C
1		SALES
2	==================
3	ALBERT	1234
4	BORIS	2345
5	CHARLES	3456
6	DENNIS	3432
7	EDNA	4321
8	FRANCIS	1321
9		------
10	TOTAL	16109

range. Similarly, if you wish to delete Francis or Albert, you can do so without obtaining the "ERROR" condition that would be the case if your range was C3...C8. After deleting or inserting a row or a column, check any formulas which use a range that included the deleted row, to be sure the formula is still valid. Print the coordinate formulas used for review, if necessary.

Forward References and Other Misfortunes

We have touched on the subject of forward references in our prior discussion of order of calculation. You will recall the problems that result when VisiCalc must reevaluate a cell before the formulas in each of its cell references are first evaluated. Our suggested cure is changing to a proper order of calculation. One can suspect that a forward reference of some sort is present when numbers change each time the [!] key is pressed. The best ways to cure the problem are to change the order of calculation with the "/GOC" or "/GOR" command, or to change the respective locations of the problem cells.

Unfortunately, forward references cannot always be cured that easily. Sometimes, overriding concerns such as ease of data entry, two uses of information located in the same cell, or limited computer memory make a planned forward reference a necessary evil. More often, however, a forward reference results from lack of advanced planning. A few recalculations resulting from the [!] key are usually sufficient to calculate properly. You know that you're done when the numbers no longer change.

The circular reference is a particularly pernicious version of the forward reference, and it is not usually cured by [!]. A circular reference occurs when two cells have formulas which refer to each other, or a single cell refers to itself. Enter the formulas

>A10: 2 * (C20)
>C20: (A10 − 3)

and see what happens when you press [!]. It is even possible to enter

>A10: (A10 + 1)

which will change each time [!] is pressed and will never give the same answer twice. This will, however, work fine until the template is reloaded onto a blank workspace. Upon reloading, cells containing such a formula will have the value "ERROR", since VisiCalc does not know what value of A10 to start with. Therefore, if you really wish A10 to add 1 to itself each time you hit [!] (to count the number of times you had to recalculate, for example), enter the formula as follows:

>A10:@IF (@ISERROR(A10),0,1 + A10)

This places a 0 in A10 if A10 was "ERROR", and adds 1 to A10 in all other cases.

There's no good way to find a circular reference, other than carefully examining the formulas in the template and trying to isolate the area in which the changing numbers seem to occur. A formula printout program, as described in Chapter 5, or a simple printout of the formulas using the "/SS" format, are much easier to work with for this purpose than a cell-by-cell examination of VisiCalc formulas on the edit line. As difficult as circular references are, however, triangular references are even worse. If Cell A1 refers to Cell B2, which refers to Cell C3, which in turn refers to Cell A1, the template may continue to change numbers with each recalculation, although an examination of the formulas involved will not show the reference problems. It can take a long while to find a triangular reference. The best way to solve the problem is to think out your template before you enter anything into your computer, and not enter the problem references into the template at all. Absent that, we suggest that you find an Adventure-playing teenager, and leave the solution to youth.

BEGINNING WITH BOOLEANS

A memory location in a digital computer usually can assume one of two states, "ON" or "OFF", or "0" or "1". These bistate conditions can also be deemed to refer to TRUE or FALSE. Values of TRUE and FALSE can also be given to certain types of variables which are used in symbolic logic. Symbolic logic is, depending upon how you look at it, either a branch of mathematics dealing with the field of logic, or a branch of logic dealing with symbolic or mathematical notation of syllogisms. This subject was developed and popularized by George Boole, a 19th-century English mathematician and logician, and is sometimes called Boolean Algebra in his honor.

The so-called Boolean values of TRUE and FALSE, and certain Boolean or Boolean-like operators, enable VisiCalc to compare two numeric variables and determine whether the first value is equal to (=), greater than (>), less than (<), greater than or equal to (=>), less than or equal to (<=), or not equal to (<>) the second value. Boolean values and operators, and various built-in Boolean functions, are important parts of most computer-programming languages, and they add considerably to the power of VisiCalc. For those readers who are unfamiliar with these concepts, a quick and (we hope) painless presentation of the subject may be in order.

We will assume a Boolean expression to be an expression which usually contains one or more of the operators = < >, and which usually has a value of TRUE or FALSE. Perhaps the simplest of the built-in Boolean functions are "@TRUE", which results in an expression which always takes the value TRUE, and "@FALSE", which will always cause a cell to assume the value FALSE. Thus, placing "@TRUE" in Cell A1 will result in the value TRUE being returned from Cell A1. Subsequent references to A1 will evaluate A1 as TRUE.

More important, we can obtain Boolean values without placing @TRUE or @FALSE in a cell. For example, the expression "1=5" has a Boolean value of FALSE, while "1<5" is TRUE. Therefore, placing "1<5" in Cell A1 will result in the same display and have the same effect as placing @TRUE in Cell A1. Similarly, if A1 and A10 have numeric values, the expression "A1<A10" placed in Cell A12 may result in a Boolean value of TRUE or FALSE. (A1 and A10 can be thought of as algebraic variables, or as the values present in the named VisiCalc cells.) Cell A12 will evaluate as TRUE, if the numeric value of A1 is equal to the numeric value of A10, or FALSE, if the values of the two variables differ. Of course, we can also compare "2*5/\12" to "17/32", and obtain a Boolean result.

Now that we can determine whether comparisons are TRUE or FALSE, we can build with these Boolean values combined with AND and OR, and their analogous built-in functions, @AND and @OR. AND, sometimes called a conjunctive operator, tests whether two conditions are each TRUE. An expression consisting of the two expressions "1=1" AND "A1=A2" is TRUE only if each of the expressions is true. This definition of AND may be shown in something called a truth table, as displayed in Figure 4.3.

One can see from this table that if each element in a row is TRUE, the "conjunction" (combination) or AND of the elements is TRUE. If any one of the elements is FALSE, the conjunction of the elements is FALSE. In VisiCalc, this conjunction is represented by the @AND built-in function. @AND(A1,B1,C1) is TRUE if A1, B1, and C1 are each TRUE, and is FALSE if any one or more of the three are FALSE.

FIGURE 4.3: AND TRUTH TABLE

A	B	C	@AND (A, B, C)
TRUE	TRUE	TRUE	TRUE
TRUE	TRUE	FALSE	FALSE
TRUE	FALSE	TRUE	FALSE
TRUE	FALSE	FALSE	FALSE
FALSE	TRUE	TRUE	FALSE
FALSE	TRUE	FALSE	FALSE
FALSE	FALSE	TRUE	FALSE
FALSE	FALSE	FALSE	FALSE

FIGURE 4.4: OR TRUTH TABLE

A	B	C	@OR (A, B, C)
TRUE	TRUE	TRUE	TRUE
TRUE	TRUE	FALSE	TRUE
TRUE	FALSE	TRUE	TRUE
TRUE	FALSE	FALSE	TRUE
FALSE	TRUE	TRUE	TRUE
FALSE	TRUE	FALSE	TRUE
FALSE	FALSE	TRUE	TRUE
FALSE	FALSE	FALSE	FALSE

A truth table for OR, somtimes called the disjunctive operator, is shown in Figure 4.4.

Once again, this disjunctive OR (which is true if and only if one, another, both, or all of the referenced elements are true) works the same way as VisiCalc's @OR built-in function. If any of the elements is TRUE, then the entire function has a value of TRUE. Only if *all* of the elements have a value of FALSE is the entire statement FALSE. Note that VisiCalc uses the standard Boolean definition of OR—the so-called nonexclusive OR—sometimes represented in overly careful legal prose as and/or, as it includes the case where each of the elements has a value of TRUE.

It may be of some interest that all of the truth tables shown in this book were designed using VisiCalc, together with the @TRUE, @FALSE, @AND, @OR, and @IF built-in functions.

This sneakily introduces us to our next topic: IF. Figure 4.5 represents a truth table showing the relationship between element A1 and element B1, with the logical formulation IF A (is TRUE), then B (is TRUE). For example, *IF* @AND(B1,B2,B3) is TRUE, *THEN* @OR(B1,B2,B3) is also TRUE.

However, if we know that @OR(B1,B2,B3) is TRUE, we really can't tell whether @AND(B1,B2,B3) is TRUE or FALSE. *IF* @AND(B1,B2,B3) is FALSE, we cannot determine, from that information alone whether @OR(B1,B2,B3) is TRUE or FALSE. *IF* we can determine whether A is TRUE, and take one action IF A is TRUE, and a different action if A is FALSE (ELSE or otherwise), we are on the way to teaching our computer program to

FIGURE 4.5: IF TRUTH TABLE

	1	2	3	4
When A is	TRUE	TRUE	FALSE	FALSE
and B is	TRUE	FALSE	TRUE	FALSE
If A, then B is	TRUE	FALSE	TRUE	TRUE

FIGURE 4.6: DECISION FLOWCHART

```
           No
  True  -------->  Action 1
   |
   | Yes
   v
 Action 2
```

make decisions. (This is represented in standard computer flowcharting, as shown in Figure 4.6.) Such graphic display makes it clear what happens when A is TRUE and what happens when A is FALSE.

The VisiCalc built-in function @IF acts much like IF, but it adds the alternative ELSE, which tells us what happens when the first argument (A) is FALSE. For example, enter the following on a blank template:

>A1:@TRUE
>A2:@IF(A1,10,20)

VisiCalc will display the number 10 in A2, IF A1 is TRUE. ELSE (that is, *IF* A1 is FALSE), 20 will be displayed. @IF permits us to substitute complex expressions for the @TRUE in A1 above. @IF takes three arguments:

1. A Boolean value (which may consist of a comparison of complex formulas).
2. A value, formula, etc. to be returned if the Boolean (first argument) evaluates to TRUE.
3. A value, formula, etc. to be returned if the Boolean evaluates to FALSE.

Cell references, complex formulas—indeed anything that will be evaluated with the Boolean value of TRUE or FALSE—can be used as arguments with @IF, and anything evaluated numerically can be returned by @IF. Not only may built-in functions such as @AND and @OR be used within these arguments, but they may be "nested" within the @IF function. For example:

>F50:@IF(B18<180000,B18*C10,@IF(B18<250000,B18*C11,
   @IF(B18<280000,B18*C12,B18*C13)))

is a perfectly legal expression, which translates as follows:

IF B18 is less than 180,000, THEN F50 equals B18 * C10
ELSE IF B18 is less than 250,000, THEN F50 equals B18 * C11
ELSE IF B18 is less than 280,000, THEN F50 equals B18 * C12
ELSE F50 equals B18 * C13

This formula, by the way, comes from a template where commissions were paid at rates specified in Cells C10, C11, C12, and C13, depending upon the various levels of sales.

More Boolean Functions

Second-stage VisiCalc contains the following Boolean functions in addition to those discussed above:

1. @NOT
2. @NA
3. @ERROR
4. @ISNA
5. @ISERROR

The @NOT function changes a value of TRUE to FALSE and vice versa. @NOT(@FALSE) is always TRUE, and @NOT(@TRUE) is always FALSE. Classically, Boolean values consisted only of TRUE and FALSE. However, VisiCalc uses the additional values of NA (not available) and ERROR. When these values are evaluated by other formulas, they are returned as NA or ERROR. If ERROR and NA are considered Boolean values, then @NA and @ERROR are Boolean functions which always return the named value. Finally, @ISERROR(*Cell*) tests *Cell* for the value ERROR, and is TRUE if *Cell* evaluates as ERROR, and otherwise FALSE. @ISNA(*Cell*) is TRUE if *Cell* is NA, and otherwise FALSE.

Use @ISERROR to test whether a cell is in an error condition. Dividing by zero, for example, results in a VisiCalc ERROR. Sometimes, however, you might wish to use such a division to result either in a 0 or in NA. A formula of the form

>A10:@IF(@ISERROR(A5),@NA,A5)

will copy A5, unless A5 is in an error condition, whereupon it will return the value @NA. The better practice, however, is to test to see if the divisor is equal to 0, and not to use @ISERROR. If A5 is equal to (A4/A3), then the formula

>A10:@IF(A3=0,@NA,A5)

will return NA. But if 0 is desired, when some information is "not available,"

>A10:@IF(A3=0,0,A5)

will do the job.

The Quasi Booleans

@IF is, to us, the most powerful of the Boolean built-in functions, but even first-stage VisiCalc carried with it a number of other functions which can make comparisons between two or more cells and return differing sets of values, depending on the results of the comparisons. While built-in functions such as @CHOOSE, @MIN, @MAX, and @LOOKUP do not really deal with TRUE and FALSE, they can often be used to good advantage in place of @IF.

@MIN and @MAX return the lowest value and highest value, respectively, of a range or list of numbers. Including a label within the range (see page 154) can sometimes confuse things, as a value of 0 may often be the smallest value in the range and could conceivably be the largest or smallest in the list. Use @MAX, for example, when you wish to subtract one number from another but desire an answer of 0 rather than a negative answer if the second is larger than the first.

$$@MAX(A1-B1,0)$$

gives the same answer as the more direct, but slightly longer to enter

$$@IF(A1>B1, A1-B1,0)$$

Another useful function is @CHOOSE.

$$@CHOOSE(n, A1,B2,17,C4,D5)$$

will return the value of the nth item in a list, where the argument "n" is the first entry after the "@CHOOSE". Thus, if n equals 3, the @CHOOSE example above will return 17; if n is equal to 5, the function will return the value of Cell D5. Note that the example is equivalent to (but much easier to type in than)

$$@IF(N<1,@NA,@IF(n=1,A1,@IF(n=2,B2,$$
$$@IF(n=3,17,@IF(n=4,C4,@IF(M=5,C5,@NA))))))$$

@LOOKUP(n, A1...A6) will do a comparison of the value of n with the values in A1 to A6 and find the cell in the range that is directly above the first cell that has a greater value than n. The function then looks at the cell in B1...B6 corresponding to the "found" cell in the A Column, and returns the value of the analogous cell. As usual, the ranges involved may be either horizontal or vertical. Thus with the number shown in Figure 4.7, the formulas

$$@LOOKUP(A1, A2...A6)$$

will yield the same results as

$$@LOOKUP(A1, C2...G2)$$

In both cases, if A1 is equal to 3, the answer will be 72.

We tended to use these quasi Booleans a lot more prior to the introduction of @IF. But these functions still often do the job as well as @IF or even better.

FIGURE 4.7

	A	B	C	D	E	F	G
1	<< >>						
2	1	24	1	2	3	4	5
3	2	48	24	48	72	96	120
4	3	72					
5	4	96					
6	5	120					

USING OVERLAYS

Overlaying worksheets can be a useful and time-saving approach to preparing templates. Overlaying is accomplished by loading two or more VisiCalc templates onto the same worksheet. In order to combine multiple templates, you simply load more than one file into VisiCalc without clearing the screen between loads. Several important rules must be remembered:

1. Data in the first loaded template will be replaced by data contained at those cell locations in the second loaded template. For example, if template 1 contains data in Cell B4, and template 2 also contains data in B4, the data in B4 of template 2 will replace the data contained in RAM for Cell B4. Of course, this technique affects only data in memory and does not alter the file as it exists on disk. The sequence

/SLOAD TEMPLATE 1
/SLOAD TEMPLATE 2

will have the results shown in Figure 4.8.

Note that the second template contained the "ITEM" labels and numbers in Column A. They were included merely to facilitate a comparison of the two templates. The second template could have contained only the value 7778 in Cell B4.

2. Data in a previously loaded template will not be eliminated by "blank" cells at the same coordinates in the overlay template currently being loaded, as shown in Figure 4.9.

Note that the data in the second template in cells B4 through B7 were inserted in the combined template without disturbing the data in Cells B1 through B3 of Template 1. Remember, the data to be overlaid from the second template must be contained in the same coordinates as they are to be entered into in the first template.

3. IF format commands are contained in otherwise blank cells, these commands will be added to labels or formulas contained in the previously loaded template, without disturbing the contents of those coordinates. Figure 4.10 illustrates the situation.

This can be a great timesaver if you must add format commands to a series of cells which already contain data you do not want to destroy. Merely save your

FIGURE 4.8

	A	B
1	ITEM 1	2334
2	ITEM 2	456
3	ITEM 3	398
4	ITEM 4	447
5	ITEM 5	6748
6	ITEM 6	765
7	ITEM 7	1110

	A	B
1	ITEM 1	
2	ITEM 2	
3	ITEM 3	
4	ITEM 4	7778
5	ITEM 5	
6	ITEM 6	
7	ITEM 7	

	A	B
1	ITEM 1	2334
2	ITEM 2	456
3	ITEM 3	398
4	ITEM 4	7778 ←
5	ITEM 5	6748
6	ITEM 6	765
7	ITEM 7	1110

existing template, clear the screen, and set up the format commands in the appropriate coordinates on the blank template. Now reload the original template. Again, remember that the second template need only contain the data, formats, or other information you want added to the template. In the example below, the format commands are shown in the square brackets.

4. Blank cells in the previously loaded template will be filled with data contained in the same coordinates in the template currently being loaded. This is basically the reverse of the examples shown in Figure 4.9 below.

There are many uses for overlaying templates. One practical application is a standard bill of material. Such an application of this technique could also apply to other areas where price lists are used. A standard price list template containing part numbers and unit prices can be prepared. This template would be updated periodically for changes in current prices. Another template, representing the bill of material or job cost sheet, would contain formulas referencing the appropriate coordinates of the price list. Alternatively, the bill of material template could reference the prices as lookup tables. Figure 4.11 shows a simplified sample price list.

FIGURE 4.9

	A	B
1	ITEM 1	4278
2	ITEM 2	3333
3	ITEM 3	2256
4	ITEM 4	
5	ITEM 5	
6	ITEM 6	
7	ITEM 7	

	A	B
1	ITEM 1	
2	ITEM 2	
3	ITEM 3	
4	ITEM 4	9328
5	ITEM 5	1476
6	ITEM 6	1212
7	ITEM 7	8787

	A	B
1	ITEM 1	4278
2	ITEM 2	3333
3	ITEM 3	2256
4	ITEM 4	9328
5	ITEM 5	1476
6	ITEM 6	1212
7	ITEM 7	8787

FIGURE 4.10

	A	B
1	ITEM 1	1222
2	ITEM 2	3239.687
3	ITEM 3	1511.1

	A	B
1	ITEM 1	[/F$]
2	ITEM 2	[/F$]
3	ITEM 3	[/F$]

	A	B
1	ITEM 1	1222.00
2	ITEM 2	3239.69
3	ITEM 3	1511.10

4: Advanced Template Design

FIGURE 4.11

	A	B
1	PART NO.	UNIT PRC
2	------	------
3	11475	21.85
4	11476	1.01
5	11477	4.56
6	11478	10.78
7	11479	5.55
8	11480	7.87
9	11481	11.35

For this example, the bill of material template containing the list of items comprising the product (exclusive of labor) might look something like Figure 4.12 when overlaid on the price list.

FIGURE 4.12

	A	B	C	D	E	F
1	PART NO.	UNIT PRC	PRODUCT #	1123		
2	------	------	BILL OF	MATERIAL		
3	11475	21.85				
4	11476	1.01	PART NO.	QUANTITY	UNIT PRC	EXTD PRC
5	11477	4.56	------	------	------	------
6	11478	10.78	11476	6	1.01	6.06
7	11479	5.55	11478	3	10.78	32.34
8	11480	7.87	11480	11	7.87	86.57
9	11481	11.35				------
10				TOTAL MATERIAL COST:		124.97

>E6:LOOKUP(C6,A3...A9)
>E6:/R:E7.E8:RNN
>F6:(D6*E6)
>F6:/R:F7.F8:RR

Of course, the replications in E6 and F6 could be carried down as far as you wish to go.

Although this is a rather simplified version of a bill of material, it illustrates the manner in which you may use this technique. Templates such as this may be used to compute numerous types of standard repetitive formulas. In addition, the simple cell references used to "pull" the pricing into the combined template may be replaced with more complex lookup and/or Boolean formulas, resulting in a more universal template.

USING DIF

In Chapter 3 we discussed the technical aspects of *how* to use VisiCalc's Data Interchange Format (DIF). In this chapter, we will show you *when* to use DIF.

FIGURE 4.13

	B	C	D	E	F
2			PREVIOUS	CURRENT	YTD
3	ITEM 1		1000	1321	2321
4	ITEM 2		110	1009	1119
5	ITEM 3		23212	2321	25533
6	ITEM 4		321	19	340
7			-------	-------	-------
8	TOTALS		24643	4670	29313

Rolling with DIF

First, consider the common requirement to "roll" statistics from the end of one month to the beginning of the next. Figure 4.13 represents a common template which has a "balance forward" in Column D, entries for the current month in Column E, and a cumulative year to date in Column F.

Each cell in column F follows the format

$$>F4:(D4 + E4)$$

Figure 4.14 shows the same template ready for the next month. Column D has last month's YTD, and Column E is blank, ready for data entry. Column F has the PREVIOUS column added to the "zeros" in Column E. The big question is, How do you get the former Column F information into Column D?

The first possibility is to replicate F to D, but this will result in circular references, as the formula "D4 + E4" is placed into D4, which again is reflected back into F. Try it and you'll see what we mean.

Next, we can move F to D, using VisiCalc's "/M" command, but this doesn't work either, as VisiCalc automatically adjusts all of the formulas, negating what you are trying to do. A move ("/M") command combined with a delete of Column D doesn't work either. VisEXEC commands can do the job, and will be discussed in the next section, but unless one is using VersaCalc 16! they are hardly simple and direct to set up, although they are very easy to use.

FIGURE 4.14

	B	C	D	E	F
2			PREVIOUS	CURRENT	YTD
3	ITEM 1		2321		2321
4	ITEM 2		1119		1119
5	ITEM 3		25533		25533
6	ITEM 4		340		340
7			-------		-------
8	TOTALS		29313		29313

4: Advanced Template Design

Finally, one could take last month's printout and simply type last month's Column F into next month's Column D. We hope that no one who has read this far will want to do it manually.

This was the "state of the art" with first-stage VisiCalc. With the introduction of DIF in second-stage VisiCalc, we can do the job directly. (Let us take this opportunity to repeat a warning. The Apple II Version 193 of VisiCalc is defective. If you use it with DIF files, you may lose the data on your disk. We think VisiCorp should give you a 202 or later version, free, but if you have to buy one, or pay an upgrade fee, do it. It's definitely worth it.)

>**F4:/S#S:ROLLOVER.DIF[RETURN]G10[RETURN][RETURN]**
>**D4:/S#L:ROLLOVER.DIF[RETURN][RETURN]**

The first line DIF-saves the appropriate portions of Columns F and G. The "totals" cells are not appropriate for DIF, and they are not really needed, because we will reload these same data back into a template which will have its own @SUMs. Remember that DIF saves values and not formulas, so that all forward-reference problems are removed. In saving not only Column F but also Column G, we are saving a group of blank cells immediately to the right of the cumulative-total cells we wish to move.

The second line DIF-loads our file into the D and E Columns, not only loading last month's cumulative totals into next month's previous column, but also blanking out last month's entries, so that Column E is fresh for entering this month's statistics.

Consolidating with DIF

A second use of DIF is in consolidating several identically formatted reports into a single "total" report. Let us assume that a retailer with stores in New York and Chicago sells three colors and four sizes of a particular item. The New York report for October, 1979, might have looked something like Figure 4.15.

The Chicago report, shown in Figure 4.16, would have the same structure, but different numbers. We would like to be able to consolidate the two reports to look like Figure 4.17.

FIGURE 4.15

	B	C	D	E
2	NEW YORK	INVENTORY	OCTOBER,1979	
3	=======	=======	=======	=======
4	COLOR	BLUE	GREEN	YELLOW
5	SIZE			
6	6	13	13	12
7	8	8	23	15
8	10	34	13	7
9	12	12	6	4
10		------	------	------
11		67	55	38

FIGURE 4.16

	B	C	D	E
2	CHICAGO	INVENTORY	OCTOBER,1979	
3	=======	=======	=======	=======
4	COLOR	BLUE	GREEN	YELLOW
5	SIZE			
6	6	10	5	3
7	8	20	12	7
8	10	30	7	5
9	12	40	3	16
10		------	------	------
11		100	27	31

Once DIF is understood, the process is simple, although the list of instructions to follow is a bit long. After a couple of runs, however, it becomes automatic.

1. DIF-save (/S#S) the Chicago data under the name *CHICAGO.DIF*. Upper left is C6 and lower right is E9. (Note that there is no good reason to save the TOTALS row, which are merely the results of @SUM formulas.)

>C6:/S#SCHICAGO.DIF[RETURN]E9[RETURN][RETURN]

2. DIF-save the New York data the same way, but with a different filename, of course.

3. Clear the screen (/CY) and enter the following commands:

>G2:(A2+D2)
>G2:/R:G3.G5:RR
>G2:/R G2.G5:H2.I2:RRRRRRRR

The result of all of this is a template which will add the contents of A2 to D2 and place it in G2; A3 and D3 and place it in G3; and so forth. Save this template (''/SS'') under the name *Consolidate*.

4. While *Consolidate* is still on the screen, DIF-load (''/S#L'') *CHICAGO.DIF*, starting in A2, and *NEWYORK.DIF* at D2.

5. After finding the totals of New York and Chicago magically appearing in the *Consolidate* section, DIF-save the *Consolidate* area under the name *TOTAL.DIF*.

FIGURE 4.17

	B	C	D	E
2	COMBINED	INVENTORY	OCTOBER,1979	
3	=======	=======	=======	=======
4	COLOR	BLUE	GREEN	YELLOW
5	SIZE			
6	6	23	18	15
7	8	28	35	22
8	10	64	20	12
9	12	52	9	20
10		------	------	------
11		167	82	69

6. Clear the screen, load a report format, without data, and DIF-load *TOTAL.DIF* into it. The result is a consolidated template which may be saved, DIF-saved, printed, or whatever else is desired.

Of course these few examples have not fully explored the capabilities of DIF. We hope that your Fear-of-DIF has been alleviated and that, as with the rest of VisiCalc, you will be able to solve your own problems with it.

VisEXEC FILES

It is often convenient to load a series of commands onto disk and have them read from the disk and executed by the computer one by one. This is a capability which is familiar to the mainframe data processor as JCL or OCL procedures, to IBM PC users as ''.BAT'' files, or to Apple users as ''Exec'' files. These files are, in effect, keyboard commands stored on diskette, which the computer will follow, just as if they were entered from the keyboard, even if you are not around.

VisiCalc does not officially support an ''exec'' capability, but most current versions of VisiCalc do have the capability of creating and following such commands. We have been warned by Software Arts, Inc., that the following is not recommended by them, and may not be available in future versions of VisiCalc. But, if your computer can use such commands, you will find them very useful. We are indebted to Jerrold H. Bents, Thomas A. Farin, and L. Darryl Mataya, authors of a program called VersaCalc! 16, who, as far as we know, were the first to document the existence of what we will call VisEXEC files.

To create a VisEXEC file, enter a series of commands into VisiCalc cell(s) as labels which are right justified. Each command must be preceded by an instruction to ''go to'' a given cell (''>Cellname''), and a '':''. In fact, you'll find that these commands look very much like an ''/SS'' printout. For example, the following might be entered in a blank VisiCalc template:

>A30:IR
>A30:IR
>G10:DC
>G10:/SL NEXTFILE

When these commands are printed to disk (''/PF'' or ''/PD'') and then loaded with the ''/SL'' command, the cell data are handled as if they were keystrokes entered directly at the keyboard. When the four lines listed above are loaded (''/SL'') into the template you wish to modify, they will move the cursor to Cell A30 and insert two rows, move the cursor to Cell G10, delete a column, and finally load NEXTFILE on top of the existing template. Note that the text must be right-justified in order for this feature to work properly.

As noted in Chapter 3, some versions of VisiCalc append a .PRF or /PRF onto filenames of print-to-disk files. If your computer uses such a convention, you cannot use your VisEXEC file without changing the name of the file from FILENAME.PRF to FILENAME.VC. (This must be done outside of VisiCalc using direct commands to your computer's operating system.)

The "page break" rows discussed elsewhere can be automated by printing the following file to disk:

>A64:/IR
>A64:/IR
>A64:/IR
>A64:/IR
>A130:/IR
>A130:/IR
>A130:/IR
>A130:/IR

When you are ready to print your multipage report (after saving the final version to disk with the "/SS" command), simply "/SL" (load) the print-to-disk file, and you will find two page breaks, each for lines wide, automatically inserted into the file.

When thinking about a VisEXEC file, you should also review the "/" language sequences at the end of your "/SS" printouts. Just about anything in those printouts, including windowing, titles, column widths, and formatting, can be included in a VisEXEC file and can be used to automatically handle your VisiCalc calculation files.

Designing a VisEXEC file takes some time to do, even with VersaCalc! 16. However, once the setup has been completed, such files are very easy to use. In the following pages we will show you how to use VisEXEC to do the same rolling from month to month that we did with DIF. We will leave it to the user to decide which technique is preferable in a given situation, but we feel it is important for the serious VisiCalc user to be familiar with both.

Rolling with VisEXEC

Let's take another look at the rollover example from the DIF portion of this chapter. You will recall the template shown in Figure 4.18.

FIGURE 4.18: MONTH ONE

	B	C	D	E	F
2			PREVIOUS	CURRENT	YTD
3	ITEM 1		1000	1321	2321
4	ITEM 2		110	1009	1119
5	ITEM 3		23212	2321	25533
6	ITEM 4		321	19	340
7			-------	-------	-------
8	TOTALS		24643	4670	29313

4: Advanced Template Design

FIGURE 4.19: MONTH TWO AFTER ADDING CURRENT MONTH'S FIGURES

	A	B	C	D	E
1				CURRENT	YTD
2	ITEM 1			1450	2321
3	ITEM 2			1212	1119
4	ITEM 3			2225	25533
5	ITEM 4			110	340
6				------	------
7	TOTALS			4997	29313

At the end of month two we enter the figures for that month in Column D. Figure 4.19 reflects the current month's data after they have been entered, but it still shows the previous month end's year-to-date (YTD) balances, in Column E.

Figure 4.20 reflects the figures at the end of month two after the print-to-disk file "UPDATE" has been loaded with the "/SS" command.

UPDATE is a print-to-disk file that contains the following:

>E2:#+D2
>E3:#+E3
>E4:#+E4
>E5:#+E6

UPDATE works as a VisEXEC file. The first line instructs VisiCalc to go to Cell E2 and pound (#) the formula at that location. This converts the contents of the cell to the value of the formula currently located in the Cell E2. VisiCalc is then instructed to add the pounded value to the value of Cell D2, the current month's figure.

Therefore, the formula 2+6 would be replaced by the value 8 when the formula was pounded. This places the formula 2,321+D2 (see Figure 4.20) at E2, and the result of this formula is the new year-to-date total of 3,771. Each successive command is then executed, so that Cells E3, E4, and E5 are also updated. When new figures are added to the CURRENT column next month, and UPDATE is loaded, the formula 2,321+D2 in Cell E2 will be pounded, resulting

FIGURE 4.20: MONTH TWO AFTER LOADING PRINT-TO-DISK FILE

	A	B	C	D	E
1				CURRENT	YTD
2	ITEM 1			1450	3771
3	ITEM 2			1212	2331
4	ITEM 3			2225	27758
5	ITEM 4			110	450
6				------	------
7	TOTALS			4997	34310

in the value 3,731, and then Cell D2 will be added to the formula. Cell E2 will then contain "3771+D2". This will continue on down to Cell E5, and this process may be used month after month to continually roll forward the monthly figures. Notice that we do not need a previous month's balance column using the VisEXEC method, whereas the DIF method does require that column in order to function properly. In addition, there are far fewer steps using the VisEXEC method once the UPDATE file has been built. Finally, a clerical worker, or other VisiCalc user, can accomplish the entire update, just by loading the one UPDATE file. Let's try another VisEXEC example.

FIGURE 4.21: FIRST PERIOD BEFORE ENTRY OF EMPLOYEES' TIME

	A	B	C	D	E	F
1						
2	JOB #1234					
3	CURRENT PERIOD TIME					
4						
5		JONES	DOE	WILSON	SMITH	TOTAL
6	TASK 1					0
7	TASK 2					0
8	TASK 3					0
9	TASK 4					0
10		--------	--------	--------	--------	--------
11		0	0	0	0	0
12						
13	JOB #1234					
14	TIME BUDGET					
15						
16		JONES	DOE	WILSON	SMITH	TOTAL
17	TASK 1	10	15	20	15	60
18	TASK 2	30	5	10	15	60
19	TASK 3	25		15	20	60
20	TASK 4	15	10		10	35
21		--------	--------	--------	--------	--------
22		80	30	45	60	215
23						
24	JOB #1234					
25	CUMULATIVE TIME TO DATE					
26						
27		JONES	DOE	WILSON	SMITH	TOTAL
28	TASK 1					0
29	TASK 2					0
30	TASK 3					0
31	TASK 4					0
32		--------	--------	--------	--------	--------
33		0	0	0	0	0
34						
35	JOB #1234					
36	TIME TO COMPLETE OR (VARIANCE)					
37						
38		JONES	DOE	WILSON	SMITH	TOTAL
39	TASK 1	10	15	20	15	60
40	TASK 2	30	5	10	15	60
41	TASK 3	25	0	15	20	60
42	TASK 4	15	10	0	10	35
43		--------	--------	--------	--------	--------
44		80	30	45	60	215
45						

More on VisEXEC

If you have ever tried to use VisiCalc as an accumulator, you probably have found out that it just doesn't work. Let's look at an actual example. Assume that you are budgeting a job which will require four workers for several time periods. At the end of each time period, you would like your secretary to enter into the template the time each employee worked during that period, taken from the employees' time reports. In addition, you want the current times to be added to the previous cumulative times to arrive at the new cumulative totals. Your template might look something like Figure 4.21.

Time for the current period is always entered in the first matrix. The total time budget is entered in the second matrix. The third matrix contains the time accumulated by the end of the previous period, plus the current-period time placed in the first matrix. The last matrix is merely the difference between the cells in the budget matrix and the corresponding cells in the cumulative matrix. Each cell in this last matrix contains a formula subtracting corresponding cells in matrix three from those in matrix two.

The employees' time for the first period will be entered in the CURRENT PERIOD TIME matrix. Figure 4.22 shows the template after the first-period time has been entered.

We now wish to add the numbers just entered to the prior period's cumulative total and place the sum in the third matrix. A file titled ACCUM.PRF has been created. This file consists of the following commands:

>B28:#+B6#
>B29:#+B7#
>B30:#+B8#
>B31:#+B9#
>C28:#+C6#
>C29:#+C7#
>C30:#+C8#
>C31:#+C9#
>D28:#+D6#
>D29:#+D7#
>D30:#+D8#
>D31:#+D9#
>E28:#+E6#
>E29:#+E7#
>E30:#+E8#
>E31:#+E9#

Once again, the "#" (pound) converts the formula contained at the cursor location to the resulting value. Thus, any formula which was in Cell B28 will be changed to its value. Then, the contents of B6 will be added to that resulting value. Finally, that resulting formula, i.e., B28 (actually the value contained therein)+B6 will be "pounded" to its resulting value. Notice that there is a

FIGURE 4.22: FIRST PERIOD AFTER ENTRY OF EMPLOYEES' TIME BUT PRIOR TO ACCUMULATION

	A	B	C	D	E	F
1						
2	JOB #1234					
3	CURRENT PERIOD TIME					
4						
5		JONES	DOE	WILSON	SMITH	TOTAL
6	TASK 1	2	4	4	5	15
7	TASK 2	3	2	4	4	13
8	TASK 3	6		3	6	15
9	TASK 4	5	2		3	10
10		--------	--------	--------	--------	--------
11		16	8	11	18	53
12						
13	JOB #1234					
14	TIME BUDGET					
15						
16		JONES	DOE	WILSON	SMITH	TOTAL
17	TASK 1	10	15	20	15	60
18	TASK 2	30	5	10	15	60
19	TASK 3	25		15	20	60
20	TASK 4	15	10		10	35
21		--------	--------	--------	--------	--------
22		80	30	45	60	215
23						
24	JOB #1234					
25	CUMULATIVE TIME TO DATE					
26						
27		JONES	DOE	WILSON	SMITH	TOTAL
28	TASK 1					0
29	TASK 2					0
30	TASK 3					0
31	TASK 4					0
32		--------	--------	--------	--------	--------
33		0	0	0	0	0
34						
35	JOB #1234					
36	TIME TO COMPLETE OR (VARIANCE)					
37						
38		JONES	DOE	WILSON	SMITH	TOTAL
39	TASK 1	10	15	20	15	60
40	TASK 2	30	5	10	15	60
41	TASK 3	25	0	15	20	60
42	TASK 4	15	10	0	10	35
43		--------	--------	--------	--------	--------
44		80	30	45	60	215

command line in the ACCUM.PRF file to add each of the corresponding coordinates of the CURRENT PERIOD TIME matrix to each of the respective coordinates of the CUMULATIVE TIME TO DATE matrix.

To update the template, load ("/SL") the ACCUM.PRF file. Each line of the file is executed as if it were keystrokes entered at the keyboard. The resulting template is shown in Figure 4.23.

We can now blank out the first period's time with another print-to-disk file, BLANK TIME.PRF, which looks like the following:

>B6:/B   >C6:/B   >D6:/B   >E6:/B
>B7:/B   >C7:/B   >D7:/B   >E7:/B
>B8:/B   >C8:/B   >D8:/B   >E8:/B
>B9:/B   >C9:/B   >D9:/B   >E9:/B

FIGURE 4.23: FIRST PERIOD AFTER ENTRY OF EMPLOYEES' TIME AND ACCUMULATION OF TIME TO DATE

	A	B	C	D	E	F
1						
2	JOB #1234					
3	CURRENT PERIOD TIME					
4						
5		JONES	DOE	WILSON	SMITH	TOTAL
6	TASK 1	2	4	4	5	15
7	TASK 2	3	2	4	4	13
8	TASK 3	6		3	6	15
9	TASK 4	5	2		3	10
10		--------	--------	--------	--------	--------
11		16	8	11	18	53
12						
13	JOB #1234					
14	TIME BUDGET					
15						
16		JONES	DOE	WILSON	SMITH	TOTAL
17	TASK 1	10	15	20	15	60
18	TASK 2	30	5	10	15	60
19	TASK 3	25		15	20	60
20	TASK 4	15	10		10	35
21		--------	--------	--------	--------	--------
22		80	30	45	60	215
23						
24	JOB #1234					
25	CUMULATIVE TIME TO DATE					
26						
27		JONES	DOE	WILSON	SMITH	TOTAL
28	TASK 1	2	4	4	5	15
29	TASK 2	3	2	4	4	13
30	TASK 3	6	0	3	6	15
31	TASK 4	5	2	0	3	10
32		--------	--------	--------	--------	--------
33		16	8	11	18	53
34						
35	JOB #1234					
36	TIME TO COMPLETE OR (VARIANCE)					
37						
38		JONES	DOE	WILSON	SMITH	TOTAL
39	TASK 1	8	11	16	10	45
40	TASK 2	27	3	6	11	47
41	TASK 3	19	0	12	14	45
42	TASK 4	10	8	0	7	25
43		--------	--------	--------	--------	--------
44		64	22	34	42	162

After this VisEXEC file has done its work, the template looks like Figure 4.24.

The cells in the TOTAL line and TOTAL column of the current period contain formulas to sum the rows and columns. Since this matrix now contains blank spaces, the sums are the zeros you see here. Also note that the cumulative-time matrix has not changed, even though the current-period matrix has been blanked. This is because our commands in the ACCUM.PRF file pounded the values in each cell in the cumulative-time matrix after referencing and adding the values in the current-time matrix. This eliminated the references to cells in the current-time matrix from the cells in the cumulative matrix.

FIGURE 4.24: FIRST PERIOD COMPLETED, WITH CURRENT-PERIOD TIME BLANKED OUT AND READY FOR ENTRY OF TIME FOR THE SECOND PERIOD

	A	B	C	D	E	F
1						
2	JOB #1234					
3	CURRENT PERIOD TIME					
4						
5		JONES	DOE	WILSON	SMITH	TOTAL
6	TASK 1					0
7	TASK 2					0
8	TASK 3					0
9	TASK 4					0
10		--------	--------	--------	--------	--------
11		0	0	0	0	0
12						
13	JOB #1234					
14	TIME BUDGET					
15						
16		JONES	DOE	WILSON	SMITH	TOTAL
17	TASK 1	10	15	20	15	60
18	TASK 2	30	5	10	15	60
19	TASK 3	25		15	20	60
20	TASK 4	15	10		10	35
21		--------	--------	--------	--------	--------
22		80	30	45	60	215
23						
24	JOB #1234					
25	CUMULATIVE TIME TO DATE					
26						
27		JONES	DOE	WILSON	SMITH	TOTAL
28	TASK 1	2	4	4	5	15
29	TASK 2	3	2	4	4	13
30	TASK 3	6	0	3	6	15
31	TASK 4	5	2	0	3	10
32		--------	--------	--------	--------	--------
33		16	8	11	18	53
34						
35	JOB #1234					
36	TIME TO COMPLETE OR (VARIANCE)					
37						
38		JONES	DOE	WILSON	SMITH	TOTAL
39	TASK 1	8	11	16	10	45
40	TASK 2	27	3	6	11	47
41	TASK 3	19	0	12	14	45
42	TASK 4	10	8	0	7	25
43		--------	--------	--------	--------	--------
44		64	22	34	42	162

4: Advanced Template Design

FIGURE 4.25: SECOND PERIOD AFTER ENTRY OF EMPLOYEES' TIME BUT PRIOR TO ACCUMULATION

	A	B	C	D	E	F
1						
2	JOB #1234					
3	CURRENT PERIOD TIME					
4						
5		JONES	DOE	WILSON	SMITH	TOTAL
6	TASK 1	4	7	12	8	31
7	TASK 2	10	4	6	7	27
8	TASK 3	10		6	12	28
9	TASK 4	12	4		6	22
10		--------	--------	--------	--------	--------
11		36	15	24	33	108
12						
13	JOB #1234					
14	TIME BUDGET					
15						
16		JONES	DOE	WILSON	SMITH	TOTAL
17	TASK 1	10	15	20	15	60
18	TASK 2	30	5	10	15	60
19	TASK 3	25		15	20	60
20	TASK 4	15	10		10	35
21		--------	--------	--------	--------	--------
22		80	30	45	60	215
23						
24	JOB #1234					
25	CUMULATIVE TIME TO DATE					
26						
27		JONES	DOE	WILSON	SMITH	TOTAL
28	TASK 1	2	4	4	5	15
29	TASK 2	3	2	4	4	13
30	TASK 3	6	0	3	6	15
31	TASK 4	5	2	0	3	10
32		--------	--------	--------	--------	--------
33		16	8	11	18	53
34						
35	JOB #1234					
36	TIME TO COMPLETE OR (VARIANCE)					
37						
38		JONES	DOE	WILSON	SMITH	TOTAL
39	TASK 1	8	11	16	10	45
40	TASK 2	27	3	6	11	47
41	TASK 3	19	0	12	14	45
42	TASK 4	10	8	0	7	25
43		--------	--------	--------	--------	--------
44		64	22	34	42	162

Now we can enter the time for the second time period. The template will look like Figure 4.25 after we enter the second period's time but before we perform the accumulate function with the ACCUM.PRF file.

We can now accumulate the time for the current period, period two, and the cumulative time as of the end of the previous period, which is currently contained in the CUMULATIVE TIME TO DATE matrix. This is accomplished by loading ("/SL") the same ACCUM.PRF file which we used at the end of the previous period. Figure 4.26 shows the template when the second period is completed.

There are other ways of accomplishing the same end result. However, they

FIGURE 4.26: SECOND PERIOD AFTER ENTRY OF EMPLOYEES' TIME AND ACCUMULATION OF TIME TO DATE

	A	B	C	D	E	F
1						
2	JOB #1234					
3	CURRENT PERIOD TIME					
4						
5		JONES	DOE	WILSON	SMITH	TOTAL
6	TASK 1	4	7	12	8	31
7	TASK 2	10	4	6	7	27
8	TASK 3	10		6	12	28
9	TASK 4	12	4		6	22
10						
11		36	15	24	33	108
12						
13	JOB #1234					
14	TIME BUDGET					
15						
16		JONES	DOE	WILSON	SMITH	TOTAL
17	TASK 1	10	15	20	15	60
18	TASK 2	30	5	10	15	60
19	TASK 3	25		15	20	60
20	TASK 4	15	10		10	35
21						
22		80	30	45	60	215
23						
24	JOB #1234					
25	CUMULATIVE TIME TO DATE					
26						
27		JONES	DOE	WILSON	SMITH	TOTAL
28	TASK 1	6	11	16	13	46
29	TASK 2	13	6	10	11	40
30	TASK 3	16	0	9	18	43
31	TASK 4	17	6	0	9	32
32						
33		52	23	35	51	161
34						
35	JOB #1234					
36	TIME TO COMPLETE OR (VARIANCE)					
37						
38		JONES	DOE	WILSON	SMITH	TOTAL
39	TASK 1	4	4	4	2	14
40	TASK 2	17	-1	0	4	20
41	TASK 3	9	0	6	2	17
42	TASK 4	-2	4	0	1	3
43						
44		28	7	10	9	54

require additional matrices to accumulate interim totals using DIF or other methods. If you are going to have another employee, such as a secretary, entering the current employee time data, the VisEXEC method is probably the simplest and quickest way to accomplish the task, once you have developed the VisEXEC files. Utilities included with VersaCalc 16! can help you in designing and implementing your VisEXEC files.

CHAPTER 5

Enhancements: Hardware and Software to Use with VisiCalc

Just as the microcomputer has spawned an industry devoted to microcomputer support, an entire subindustry has developed to support users of VisiCalc. Hardware and software developers have jumped on the bandwagon and entered the market with enhancements to use with VisiCalc and VisiCalc files. These hardware and software peripherals include:

- Random Access Memory (RAM) expansions to increase VisiCalc's available workspace.
- Software and hardware to permit an 80-column upper- and lower-case display for machines designed only for 40-column upper-case display.
- Planning sheets and software to assist with VisiCalc template design and debugging.
- Software to prepare VisiCalc data and to manipulate VisiCalc data files for further use or for use by other programs.

We'll explore some of the more useful of these here.

Software Enhancements

VERSACALC 16!. VersaCalc 16! consists of a disk and a large manual with instructions on using VisEXEC files as discussed in Chapter 4. Although VersaCalc! was initially written for the Apple II, the principles it explains are just as applicable to other equipment. However, the degree to which various functions work on different versions of VisiCalc will vary.

VersaCalc! includes a tutorial, which fully explains the use of the VisEXEC feature. It also has a utility disk containing VisiCalc files which can be used to simplify the building of these print-to-disk VisEXEC files. In the Apple II version, VersaCalc! also includes an Applesoft program, which will take the data from a VisiCalc print-to-disk file and sort the items in ascending or descending order. The data can be a row or column of VisiCalc labels or numbers, but the data from only one row or column may be used as the sort field. VersaCalc! then prepares a new file containing a series of GoTo coordinates and MOVE commands, which moves entire columns or rows within a VisiCalc template into the proper order right before your very eyes. VersaCalc! eliminates much of the tedious work required to create complex VisEXEC files, and it is a must for the serious VisiCalc user.

PLANNING AND DEBUGGING. By now you are familiar with our philosophy that VisiCalc is really a programming language and should be treated as such. This means that the logic of your work should be put to paper before turning on the computer. A VisiCalc coding sheet, which can be used to record your plan, as well as document what you did, is extremely useful when working with any but the smallest templates.

CalcPad is a relatively new product, which is not a keypad but instead a pad of specially printed 11-by-17-inch sheets of paper. CalcPad is, in effect, a VisiCalc coding sheet, with space for showing replications, report areas, global formats, template overlays, and all of the other planning methods which have been discussed elsewhere in this book. Intended to be used both beforehand for template design, and afterwards for template documentation, CalcPad will remind you of the decisions you have to make when designing a template, and it will certainly save you a lot of time with your template design. Even with CalcPad, it is often very helpful to see a printout of your template, not in the /SS or /PF form, but with full formula printout, in a templatelike grid format. Several programs for the Apple and IBM versions of VisiCalc do the job, but our current favorite is DocuCalc. Figures 5.1, 5.2, and 5.3 show the same small template in a standard printout form, a "/SS" printout, and a printout written by DocuCalc. Note how much easier it is to "read" and understand the DocuCalc printout. Several options are available which allow you to print the model in grid format or one formula per line in alphanumeric ascending order. DocuCalc will also provide you with a listing of all forward references.

DATA SHARING WITH OTHER PROGRAMS. It often happens that data are available in a form not directly usable by VisiCalc. For example, one might obtain stock quotations from the Dow Jones News Retrieval Service (see Figure 5.4) and wish to manipulate the closing price and volume information in a VisiCalc template designed for stock analysis. The obvious option is to print out the information and enter it into the VisiCalc template by hand, but that adds a lot of work which should be unnecessary.

The better answer is to utilize a program which will read a DJNS file and

FIGURE 5.1

	A	B	C	D	E	F	G
1	STUDENT	EXAM #1	EXAM #2	EXAM #3	FINAL EXM	TOTAL	AVERAGE
2							
3	ANDY	93	97	88	91	460	92.00
4	BETTY	77	89	71	70	377	75.40
5	CHARLOTTE	99	100	98	99	495	99.00
6	DAVID	60	70		74	278	69.50
7	EDNA	69	75	79	89	401	80.20
8	GEORGE	91	91	91	95	463	92.60
9	HOWARD	79			99	277	92.33
10	ILENE	98	98	98		294	58.80
11		------	------	------	------	------	------
12	AVERAGES	83.25	88.57	87.50	88.14	380.63	82.48

convert the quotations into a format readable by VisiCalc, most likely a DIF format. Most of the programs which accomplish this feat permit you to isolate the required data by hand in the "free form" text file but also permit you to specify certain fields in the input file, if it is a bit more structured.

Finally, many data-base-management programs both read and write DIF files. This feature, with a bit of preparation, will allow you to utilize information stored in your data base by reading it into VisiCalc. Then, if you like, you may write it back to the data base in altered form. These are obviously the uses for which DIF was designed. Unfortunately, DIF has not become a universal file structure. If you are selecting a data-base program, however, the ability to read and write DIF files is a feature that may be important to you.

CONSOLIDATING AND OTHER MANIPULATIONS. One of Visi-Calc's weaknesses is the inability to do direct consolidations of several templates with the same format, into a template which totals, compares, or ranks its various components. We have explained, in Chapter 4, one way of doing consolidations using DIF. However, it is also possible to develop programs in BASIC or some other language which will read your VisiCalc files and manipulate them.

Several programs currently on the market for various computers will allow you to re-form print-to-disk or DIF files from one specified column width to several columns of another specified width—e.g., one can divide one 36-character column into four 9-character columns or vice versa. You can also take standard Apple textfiles, even those downloaded from another computer, and transform them into standard VisiCalc textfiles which will reload into a VisiCalc template beginning at the coordinate location you specify. At least one of these packages contains a communication program as well, to allow you to access another computer for the data.

Another program will allow you to relocate rows or columns of data from one area of a template to another area. You may also write a single VisiCalc file comprised of several files and vice versa.

There are a variety of programs which will allow you to use a VisiCalc print-to-disk or DIF file to print a template comprised of columns having differ-

FIGURE 5.2

```
>G12:/F$@AVERAGE(G2...G11
>F12:/F$@AVERAGE(F2...F11
>E12:/F$@AVERAGE(E2...E11
>D12:/F$@AVERAGE(D2...D11
>C12:/F$@AVERAGE(C2...C11
>B12:/F$@AVERAGE(B2...B11
>A12:"AVERAGES
>G11:"  ------
>F11:"  ------
>E11:"  ------
>D11:"  ------
>C11:"  ------
>B11:"  ------
>G10:/F$(F10)/(@COUNT(B10...D10)+2)
>F10:@SUM(B10...D10)+(2*E10)
>D10:98
>C10:98
>B10:98
>A10:"ILENE
>G9:/F$(F9)/(@COUNT(B9...D9)+2)
>F9:@SUM(B9...D9)+(2*E9)
>E9:99
>B9:79
>A9:"HOWARD
>G8:/F$(F8)/(@COUNT(B8...D8)+2)
>F8:@SUM(B8...D8)+(2*E8)
>E8:95
>D8:91
>C8:91
>B8:91
>A8:"GEORGE
>G7:/F$(F7)/(@COUNT(B7...D7)+2)
>F7:@SUM(B7...D7)+(2*E7)
>E7:89
>D7:79
>C7:75
>B7:69
>A7:"EDNA
>G6:/F$(F6)/(@COUNT(B6...D6)+2)
>F6:@SUM(B6...D6)+(2*E6)
>E6:74
>C6:70
>B6:60
>A6:"DAVID
>G5:/F$(F5)/(@COUNT(B5...D5)+2)
>F5:@SUM(B5...D5)+(2*E5)
>E5:99
>D5:98
>C5:100
>B5:99
>A5:"CHARLOTTE
>G4:/F$(F4)/(@COUNT(B4...D4)+2)
>F4:@SUM(B4...D4)+(2*E4)
>E4:70
>D4:71
>C4:89
>B4:77
>A4:"BETTY
>G3:/F$(F3)/(@COUNT(B3...D3)+2)
>F3:@SUM(B3...D3)+(2*E3)
>E3:91
>D3:88
>C3:97
>B3:93
>A3:"ANDY
>G1:" AVERAGE
>F1:"  TOTAL
>E1:"FINAL EXM
>D1:"EXAM #3
>C1:"EXAM #2
>B1:"EXAM #1
>A1:"STUDENT
/W1
/GOC
/GRM
/GC9
/X-/X>A1:>D14:
```

ent widths. For example, Column A could be 3 characters wide, Column B could be 20 characters, Columns C through H might be 12 characters each, and Column I might be 4 characters wide.

And finally, there are programs which will sort VisiCalc files. With any of these programs it is necessary to save a VisiCalc file of some type (usually a /PF or DIF file), get out of VisiCalc, and run the manipulation program, which will ultimately save a file or files that VisiCalc can read. If the VisiCalc file was a /PF file, the peripheral software probably prints the report; if the VisiCalc file was a DIF file, the peripheral program is likely to save a DIF file, which can then be read back into VisiCalc and printed or recalculated.

Good sources of information are the documentation and product reviews in various magazines having columns specializing in VisiCalc matters. We advise that you read them thoroughly so as to select the programs most appropriate for your application. And of course, the value of a friendly and knowledgeable computer store salesperson cannot be overestimated. These programs may not only assist you in accomplishing what you want to do, but may help you to

FIGURE 5.3

	A	B	C	D	E	F	G
1	STUDENT	EXAM #1	EXAM #2	EXAM #3	FINAL EXM	TOTAL	AVERAGE
2							
3	ANDY	93	97	88	91	@SUM(B3...D3)+(2*E3)	(F3)/(@COUNT(B3...D3)+2)
4	BETTY	77	89	71	70	@SUM(B4...D4)+(2*E4)	(F4)/(@COUNT(B4...D4)+2)
5	CHARLOTTE	99	100	98	99	@SUM(B5...D5)+(2*E5)	(F5)/(@COUNT(B5...D5)+2)
6	DAVID	60	70		74	@SUM(B6...D6)+(2*E6)	(F6)/(@COUNT(B6...D6)+2)
7	EDNA	69	75	79	89	@SUM(B7...D7)+(2*E7)	(F7)/(@COUNT(B7...D7)+2)
8	GEORGE	91	91	91	95	@SUM(B8...D8)+(2*E8)	(F8)/(@COUNT(B8...D8)+2)
9	HOWARD	79			99	@SUM(B9...D9)+(2*E9)	(F9)/(@COUNT(B9...D9)+2)
10	ILENE	98	98	98		@SUM(B10...D10)+(2*E10)	(F10)/(@COUNT(B10...D10)+2)
11		------	------	------	------	------	------
12	AVERAGES	@AVERAGE(B2...B11)	@AVERAGE(C2...C11)	@AVERAGE(D2...D11)	@AVERAGE(E2...E11)	@AVERAGE(F2...F11)	@AVERAGE(G2...G11)
13							

understand much more about VisiCalc itself. The techniques which you will learn from these programs can provide you with the means to further your own abilities with VisiCalc.

TALKING TO OTHER COMPUTERS. VisiCalc files, being standard textfiles, can be transferred from one computer to another in the same way as any other textfile. The method most common in the microcomputer world connects two computers by means of a telephone line and a modem. A modem is a device which, when connected to the sending computer, converts the electrical impulses in the computer to *mod*ulated audio tones on the telephone line, and when connected to a receiving computer, *dem*odulates the audio tones and converts them to electrical impulses directly usable by the computer.

FIGURE 5.4

DOW JONES STOCK QUOTE REPORTER SERVICE.
STOCK QUOTES DELAYED OVER 15 MINUTES
*=CLOSE PRICE ADJUSTED FOR EX-DIVIDEND

STOCK	BID CLOSE	ASKED OPEN	HIGH	LOW	LAST	VOL(100'S)
AAPL	60 3/8	60 1/2				4808
OTU	41 1/4	41 1/4	41 1/4	41 1/4	41 1/4	79
CNCPF	2 1/8	2 1/4				22
CSC	17 7/8	18	18	17 3/4	18	495
IBM	112 1/2	113 1/8	115	113	114 5/8	6654

	A	B	C	D	E	F	G
1		CLOSE	OPEN	HIGH	LOW	LAST	VOL(100'S
2	AAPL	60.38	60.50				4808
3	OTU	41.25	41.25	41.25	41.25	41.25	79
4	CNCPF	2.13	2.25				22
5	CSC	17.88	18.00	18.00	17.75	18.00	495
6	IBM	112.50	113.13	115.00	113.00	114.63	6654

As long as both computers recognize the same codes as standing for the same characters, they can talk to each other even if operating systems, programming languages, microprocessor chips, and the like are different. Most if not all of the microcomputers use ASCII format and should be able to talk to each other. With the appropriate MODEM software, VisiCalc DIF files or VisiCalc templates can be transferred from an Apple II to a Radio Shack Model III; the template file will then "run" on the Model III without change, making VisiCalc, as a programming language, at least as portable as a program written in BASIC or Pascal.

Occasionally, slight technical differences between computers do create problems. The IBM PC, for example, requires a line feed symbol after each carriage return; the Apple II operating system knows that a line feed is required after each carriage return and does not require the line feed to actually be present. Therefore, when transferring a program from an Apple II to an IBM PC, the user must somehow convert each carriage return into a carriage return–line feed sequence, to assist the IBM in understanding what it is getting. We suggest that a word processor search-and-replace function (see below) is the easiest way to do this. Once the line feed problem is solved, however, the VisiCalc file will run on the IBM computer in exactly the same way as it worked in the Apple.

Note, however, that the VisiCalc versions in both machines must have the same features. Or at the very least, the sending machine must not use features that the receiving machine's VisiCalc does not have. We have found that, except for file size and a feature on Hewlett Packard versions, the current, standard VisiCalc available is the same for all the machines that we have tested. The Hewlett Packard feature is that VisiCalc designed for the HP machines utilizes an algebraic hierarchy of calculation, rather than the simple left-to-right calculation in all other versions. Transfer to and from HP computers, therefore, may require insertion of parentheses to force calculation to get the intended method result.

GRAPHING PROGRAMS. VisiCalc has what is laughingly referred to as a graph format, which enables the user to develop extremely rudimentary horizontal bar charts, using asterisks. Obviously such graphics won't do for sophisticated uses of any type, and it is preferable to use a graphing program which utilizes VisiCalc data saved with the DIF function in order to present the data in graphs and statistical analyses.

The first of these programs was VisiPlot, which, together with its companion VisiTrend, is sold by VisiCorp. VisiPlot reads DIF files and uses them as data for graphs per parameters specified by the user. Once again, however, it is necessary to DIF-save the file, terminate VisiCalc, run VisiPlot, and read the previously saved DIF file back in. Although often relatively slow (when compared to VisiCalc itself) such graphing programs commonly enable the user to output VisiCalc data in a form easily assimilated by the intended audience.

An obvious "visitrend," at the time this is being written, is towards graphing programs integrated with spreadsheet programs, so that tables or graphs will be considered two interchangeable viewing modes of the same data. The user will be able to switch from one to the other viewing mode quickly, without trouble.

At this writing, such capability is more or less available with Lotus Development Corporation's program "1-2-3" for the IBM PC and others, Apple Computer's LISA computer, and Context Management Systems' MBA.

WORD PROCESSOR INTERFACES. The chances are excellent that any standard word-processing program using the same operating system as your VisiCalc textfiles, and using standard ASCII files, can be used to edit and manipulate VisiCalc files which have been saved or printed to disk. Global or location-by-location search and replace, and your word processor's other editing functions, can be used to speed up the modification of your templates. In addition, with the right word processor you can incorporate the report portions of the template into the text of your formal reports, so that they can be printed as part of the document.

ENHANCED VISICALC FEATURES. Although VisiCorp and Software Arts may not like it, several companies have announced "preboot" programs which will modify VisiCalc as it is read in by your computer. They can add to your VisiCalc, on the fly, such features as special formats, variable column widths, and utilization of expanded memory. We believe that, as new features become available in other spreadsheets, preboot manufacturers will attempt to supply these features to users of "old" VisiCalc, particularly if VisiCorp refuses to add the new features itself, with reasonably priced updates.

Hardware Enhancements

Possibly the most significant advance for the VisiCalc user has been the development of RAM expansion boards. With the Apple II with standard 48K of memory, the VisiCalc user had only 18K of workspace. Adding an additional 16K memory expansion board gave the VisiCalc user 34K of space. Similarly, a standard 64K IBM PC made only 22K of workspace available, while a standard expansion to 128K permitted templates of 86K. Unfortunately, TRS-80 memory expansions are not common, and the 18K available with Model III VisiCalc is simply too small for serious work.

In addition to the Apple 16K expansion board, 32K, 64K, and 128K RAM expansion boards manufactured by Saturn Systems, Inc., and others have become common. These RAM expansion boards in conjunction with a software preboot can modify VisiCalc, in RAM, to allow it to utilize these memory boards to increase the size of your available workspace. With these products you may use multiple RAM boards with the Apple II in order to obtain up to 176K or more of usable space, which can be saved on multiple diskettes in consecutively numbered files.

Many 80-column output boards to double the number of characters per line on the Apple II are available, and the manufacturers of most of these boards provide preboots to enable VisiCalc to be displayed in 80 columns. Because of the way the 80-column boards work, the user will notice a slower "scrolling" speed, but the larger display can be well worth it. VisiCalc for the Apple //e with a built-in 80-column card provides 80-column display, without any preboot, as the //e is treated as an 80-column display computer, just like the Apple /// or IBM PC.

If you are good with data entry into an adding machine, a numeric keypad like that on an adding machine will speed up data entry significantly. For those of you whose computer does not have a built-in keypad (or for you IBM PC owners who would rather "scroll" than use the keypad), add-ons are available. In addition to the normal 10 numeric keys and a decimal-point key, a good keypad for use with VisiCalc should have at least the following keys: +, −, ←, →, [RETURN], [ESCAPE] and [SPACE]. Additional keys such as (,), *, and / are helpful. However, a 10-key (or 11-key) keypad without the additional function keys is inadequate, since you will find yourself moving between the keypad and the keyboard in order to enter data, move the cursor, and change the cursor direction.

One last hardware enhancement, for the Apple II computer, is the Videx Keyboard Enhancer. This product, together with a Videx-supplied preboot and an 80-column board, not only gives the Apple user the ability to enter labels in lower- as well as upper-case, but also permits storage of keyboard "macros" such as ">A1", "/\CI132N", or "/SLLONGFILENAME". This macro feature can also be used to set up a lengthy printer setup string in as few as one or two keystrokes. One must suspect that new versions of VisiCalc tailored to the Apple //e will do these jobs without the need for a keyboard enhancer.

Additional hardware and software enhancements for use with VisiCalc are entering the marketplace quite regularly. The addition of selected hardware and software enhancements to VisiCalc and/or your computer, and the printing and file-saving techniques described above, should add even more to your ability to design and present meaningful reports with a professional appearance.

CHAPTER 6

Designing an Application

The aspect of VisiCalc most important to you as a businessman, a manager, or just an individual with financial or mathematical problems is the variety of practical applications that it can help you solve. To illustrate this point, we will develop a scenario similar to one you may encounter in your own day-to-day responsibilities. Even if you have no use for this particular application, the techniques employed in designing this template will provide you with the skills to use VisiCalc more effectively.

Our scenario begins in a frantic rush, as such things usually do. You own A & A Products, Inc., a modest-sized business, which distributes three products. You have an opportunity to expand your business into other areas of the country. However, expansion will require additional capital. You have discussed your needs with your banker, and he is supportive of your enthusiasm. However, he is—alas—a banker at heart and he wants proof that you do not need the loan before he will advance any funds. You impress upon him the need for speed in this undertaking, since your exclusive on the distribution rights in this new territory will expire in one week. He responds by informing you that he will be leaving town in three days for a one-month vacation, and he would have to approve the loan before he leaves. What little time you thought you had has now been cut in half.

Your banker has requested a forecast, by month, for the next year. He has asked to see projected statements of income, projected balance sheets, and projected statements of cash flow. How are you going to meet the deadline? You could sit down and prepare manual worksheets and insert all the necessary data and then make all the required calculations on your brand new financial calculator. You might be able to get it calculated, typed, proofread, and corrected before your banker left town. But he wants, not only your most optimistic estimates, but estimates based upon "worst case" assumptions as well.

Well, you could put the basic data on your worksheets and projected financial statements and then photocopy these repetitive sheets. Then each set of sheets could be used to develop the calculations for a new set of assumptions. Of course, you would have to make all the calculations for each of the scenarios. Your secretary would then type the statements and you would proofread them. If you found any computational errors in your work or in the typing, all or a substantial number of the scenarios would have to be recalculated, retyped, and reproofed. You could probably finish these projections by the time your banker returned from vacation, long after your option expired.

If your business is large enough to have a mainframe or a minicomputer, you could have your data-processing department develop a program to do the work for you. The project could then be finished when your banker returned from his vacation next year. This is not meant to downplay the importance or competence of data-processing professionals. It merely reflects the realities of life. Program development requires substantial quantities of time, and running the day-to-day business of the corporation does have its priorities.

The "personal" computer, and applications software such as VisiCalc, have totally changed the way many executives, professionals, and middle managers do business today. The resources to solve these everyday emergencies as well as the less urgent repetitive problems are now available at a relatively small cost.

Let's look at how we can construct a template using VisiCalc to provide the data required by our banker and at the same time provide us with a working model which may be used for our own internal budgeting and forecasting.

As always, it is necessary to understand your business problem before solving it with VisiCalc. For those of you with little or no financial or accounting background, we provide here a basic review of the financial statements we will use in the template and a discussion of what these statements represent. For purposes of our discussion, we will include in the category of financial statements the balance sheet, statement of income, and statement of cash flow.

The balance sheet, sometimes called a statement of financial position, is a statement which reflects the amounts of a business' assets, liabilities, and ownership equity at a point in time. Assets are property owned by the business that will provide a benefit to some future period. Cash in bank, furniture and fixtures, and merchandise inventory are examples of assets. A liability is an obligation incurred in connection with the acquisition of an asset or the incurring of an expense. A long-term bond and an unpaid telephone bill are examples of liabilities. Owners' equity is the cumulative capital contributed, or invested, by the owners of the business, plus the cumulative earnings of the business to date, less any losses of the business to date. For the uninitiated, the basic accounting equation is:

Assets = Liabilities + Owners' equity

Or, if you prefer, one may state the equation as

$$\text{Assets} - \text{Liabilities} = \text{Owners' equity.}$$

The statement of income is a list of the income and expenses of the business for a period of time, such as January 1, 1983, through and including December 31, 1983. Income accounts represent the amounts of income earned during the period. Expense accounts reflect the amounts of expenditures incurred during the period. Generally, these expenses are incurred in order to earn income. However, expenses may be incurred when no income is earned.

The statement of cash flow reflects actual cash received and paid out during the period, as opposed to income earned and expenses incurred. When a sale is consummated and title passes to the buyer, income is generally "earned," even though the cash sales price has not yet been received. When merchandise is purchased, a cost or expense has been incurred even though it has not been paid for. Why, you may ask, should I provide my banker with both a statement of income and a statement of cash flow? Simply because profits, reflected in the statement of income, will not help you pay your bills if the cash is not in the bank. Similarly, we have not discussed the statement of changes in financial position, required in accordance with generally accepted accounting principles, since the banker will probably be more interested, at this time, in the projected statement of cash flow in order to evaluate the borrower's ability to repay the loan.

The balance sheet, then, lists these assets and liabilities as well as ownership equity; the statement of income lists the income earned and expenses incurred; and the statement of cash flow lists the actual cash receipts and cash outlays, which may be quite different from the earnings and expenses.

Although this discussion has provided you with only a brief overview of financial statements, you should now have enough information to appreciate the problem that we'll discuss.

A & A Products distributes three principal products, which we'll call A, B, and C. These products are seasonal. Products A and C are warm-weather products, while product B is a cold-weather product. The seasons relate generally to the calendar quarters. In order to provide adequate product for the warm weather, several months of production lead time are necessary. However, during the warm season, less labor and lead time are required to prepare for the upcoming winter season and to maintain current production.

We'll also assume that operating expenses fall into three basic categories: those related directly to payroll, those related to sales, and those which can be estimated in amount rather than as a percent of sales or payroll, since they are fixed. Operating expenses are not expected to increase significantly over the next 12 months due to inflationary factors. However, they will fluctuate based upon sales and production levels. Direct costs of production, that is, costs of sales, can be estimated as a percentage of sales price, by product.

Furthermore, it is assumed that there is sufficient historical data available to estimate financial ratios relative to accounts receivable collection periods, inventory requirements, and other financial aspects of the company.

The template as illustrated here contains only the first quarter's data and formulas. It requires 10 columns and 253 rows and consumes approximately 30K of workspace. A complete year requires substantially more space. Although such a large model will not fit in all computers, it has been used here as an example in order to demonstrate a wide variety of VisiCalc's features. The example contains all of the data and results as reflected in the final template. However, in reality you would first build a "blank" template which would be saved on disk prior to data entry. An example of this blank template is contained in Appendix C. In order to utilize column widths narrow enough to allow for the printing of the report on standard computer paper, or on conventional paper in letter-quality printers, the amounts have been rounded to thousands of dollars.

We have included as many examples of VisiCalc techniques as possible in the model in order to demonstrate their use. Many of the calculations could be performed using these or other techniques, and the model could be made more efficient. However, for purposes of illustration, we have taken this lengthier route. A grid containing the actual cell contents—i.e., labels, formulas, and numbers rather than the results of the calculations—is included as Appendix D. This grid was printed using DocuCalc, described in further detail in Chapter 5.

Let's discuss the background and basic assumptions, the detailed formulas, and a bit of the accounting theory necessary to construct our model. The first portion of the template is an input area which contains all of the data, including variables, necessary for the calculation of the projected statement of income. Figure 6.1 contains the first portion of the template, the user input and interim calculation area.

Rows 15 through 85 of Figure 6.1 require input by the user, and Rows 87 through 94 contain interim computations resulting from this input. These interim results are used in further calculations elsewhere in the template and could actually be made within the body of the projected statement of income. However, this could require complex forward references, described in Chapter 4, which would necessitate multiple recalculations of the template in order to obtain the proper results. As discussed elsewhere, whenever workspace (memory) permits, interim calculations should be made in order to avoid such forward references.

As another illustration of the techniques described throughout the book, various items requiring only value inputs are included in this portion of the template. At first glance, this design appears to require needless duplication of simple data which could be input just as easily into the body of the report itself. However, by including the data here in a separate "User Input" portion of the template, all data entry required of the user is in one easy-to-find location. Thus the user need not search through the entire template looking for items requiring data input. This form of organization also helps eliminate the possibility that an inexperienced user will enter data in areas containing formulas or other information required for the proper calculation of the template. Memory limitations may preclude this luxury, since this technique requires extra workspace. However, with the memory expansion systems now available for the Apple II, as discussed in Chapter 5, and the advent of the expanded Apple /// (256K) and the IBM Personal Computer, this technique should be usable in many cases.

Before we begin the template, we first enter the applicable global data. In this case, the global commands are as follows:

Column width = 8 (/GC8)

Order of recalculation = Columnar (/GOC)

Recalculation mode = Manual (/GRM)

Format = General (/GFG)

Now, let's look at the actual formulas and the data entry required in this first portion of the template. Row 17 contains the numbers of the months—e.g., 1 for January and 2 for February—at the tops of the respective columns. The month numbers, rather than names, are used here so that we may reference these values for use in numerous formulas throughout the template. Using IF/THEN/ELSE, @LOOKUP, and @CHOOSE functions, these formulas will perform different tasks depending upon the month for which the calculation is performed. The quarter code on Row 18 represents the fiscal quarter for each respective month. January through March contain a 1, April through June would contain a 2, and so forth. These factors may be entered by the designer rather than the user.

Next, seasonal factors are entered. The Lookup Code, on Row 23, represents the number of the first month in each of the fiscal quarters. The season code, on Row 24, contains the number, 1 through 4, of the quarter/season. These codes will be used in connection with formulas which will relate the appropriate season code to the corresponding factors for the respective seasons. The quarter code described above could have been used as well. However, the lookup code is used here in order to demonstrate an alternative approach.

Rows 25 through 30 reflect the seasonal factors for the three products and the various expenses which are affected by seasonal fluctuations. Notice that the local format has been set to the "$" format in this area in order to improve the appearance of the displayed data. The monthly inflation rate is entered in the "$" format as well on Row 31. The "</F$>" in Column D on Rows 25 through 31 is a reminder to the user that the data are to be displayed in the "$" format. If you will be using percentages having three or more decimal places, you may want to use the general format for display purposes.

Notice that the seasonal data represent percentages ranging from 94 to 115. It is assumed that the greatest sales effort and the related costs are associated with products A and C. Consequently, additional expenditures are related directly to the increased sales level of these products in the first and second quarters of the year. In addition, some preparation for this sales period is required, while less is needed toward the latter portion of the period. Hence, we must include lead and lag time in our calculations. Therefore, payroll in the fourth quarter of one year and in the first quarter of the subsequent year will be higher than in other periods

FIGURE 6.1: FIRST USER INPUT AREA

```
    A      B     C     D     E       F        G        H        I
 1
 2        A & A PRODUCTS, INC.
 3        1984 FINANCIAL PROJECTIONS
 4
 5   >>>>>>>>>>>>>>>>>>>>>  U S E R   I N P U T  <<<<<<<<<<<<<<<<<<<<<<<
 6   >                           A N D                                 <
 7   >             I N T E R I M   C A L C U L A T I O N S             <
 8   >                                                                 <
 9   >  _____                 <
10   >  >> I N P U T   B Y   U S E R <<<<<                              <
11   >  _____                         <
12   >                                                                 <
13   >                                       1984                      <
14   >                                 ----------------------          <
15   >  MONTH/SEASON CONVERSION        JAN.    FEB.    MAR.            <
16   >  -----------------------        ------  ------  ------          <
17   >  MONTH NUMBER                     1       2       3             <
18   >  FISCAL QUARTER CODE              1       1       1             <
19   >                                                                 <
20   >                         BASIS                                   <
21   >  SEASONAL FACTORS       CODE  1ST QTR 2ND QTR 3RD QTR 4TH QTR   <
22   >  ----------------       -----  ------  ------  ------  ------   <
23   >  LOOKUP CODE                     1       4       7      10      <
24   >  SEASON CODE                     1       2       3       4      <
25   >  PAYROLL (P/R)    </F$>    1   1.03    0.97    0.99    1.10     <
26   >  SALES RELATED(SL </F$>    2   1.07    1.02    0.97    0.99     <
27   >  OTHER [CODE#3]   </F$>    3   1.03    1.01    0.97    0.99     <
28   >  SALES, PRODUCT A </F$>    4   1.10    1.15    0.97    0.95     <
29   >  SALES, PRODUCT B </F$>    5   0.98    0.94    1.08    1.10     <
30   >  SALES, PRODUCT C </F$>    6   1.07    1.12    0.99    0.96     <
31   >  MONTHLY INFLTN RATE</F$>  1.00-                                 <
32   >                                                                 <
33   >  PRODUCT MIX:                   JAN.    FEB.    MAR.   TOTAL    <
34   >  ------------                  ------  ------  ------  ------   <
35   >  PROD-A UNITS                  10000   11000   12100   33100    <
36   >         SLS PRICE                 40      40      40            <
37   >         COST %                    .7      .7    .675            <
38   >  PROD-B UNITS                  20000   19600   19208   58808    <
39   >         SLS PRICE                 36      36      36            <
40   >         COST %                    .8      .8      .8            <
41   >  PROD-C UNITS                 100000  107000  114490  321490    <
42   >         SLS PRICE                  3       3       3            <
43   >         COST %                    .6    .575    .565            <
44   >                                                                 <
45   >                         BASIS                                   <
46   >  OPERATING RATIOS & INPUT CODE                                   <
47   >  ------------------------ -----                                  <
48   >  SALARIES, OFFICERS         7    24                              <
49   >  SALARIES, OFFICE          10    30                              <
50   >  SALARIES, SALES            1    20                              <
51   >  PAYROLL TAXES              8   .08                              <
52   >  ADVERTISING                2  .015                              <
53   >  BAD DEBT EXPENSE           2  .015                              <
54   >  COMMISSIONS                2   .03                              <
55   >  DELIVERY                   2  .014                              <
56   >  DEPRECIATION               9     9                              <
57   >  GROUP INSURANCE            8   .08                              <
58   >  INSURANCE                  3     8                              <
59   >  INTEREST              (NOTES)  .15                              <
60   >  LEGAL & ACCOUNTING         7     5                              <
61   >  MOTOR VEHICLE EXPENSE      3     4                              <
62   >  OFFICE SUPPLIES & EXPNS    3     4                              <
63   >  RENT                       9     4                              <
64   >  REPAIRS & MAINTENANCE      3     5                              <
65   >  SELLING                    2  .008                              <
66   >  TAXES, OTHER               3     2                              <
67   >  TELEPHONE                  3     3                              <
68   >  TRADE SHOWS                2  .003                              <
69   >  TRAVEL                     2  .004                              <
```

```
     A      B         C         D        E        F        G        H        I
 70  >  INCOME TAXES                  (IBIT)      .44                               <
 71  >                                                                              <
 72  >  FINANCIAL RATIOS:                                                           <
 73  >  ----------------                                                            <
 74  >  INVENTORY DAYS                             28                               <
 75  >  CASH DAYS IN OPRTNG EXPS                   60                               <
 76  >  ACCOUNTS RECEIVABLE DAYS                   45                               <
 77  >  ACCOUNTS PAYABLE DAYS                      35                               <
 78  >  ACCRUED EXPENSES DAYS                      30                               <
 79  >                                                                              <
 80  >  OTHER DATA:                                                                 <
 81  >  -----------                                                                 <
 82  >  PROPERTY, PLANT & EQUIP.                   10        10       10            <
 83  >  NOTE PAYABLE ADDITIONS                      0         0        0            <
 84  >  LONG TERM DEBT ADDITIONS                    0         0        0            <
 85  >  LONG TERM DEBT REPAYMENTS                   3         3        3            <
 86  >                                                                              <
 87  >  >> C O M P U T E D   F I E L D S <<<<<<<<                                   <
 88  >                                                                              <
 89  >  ---------------------------------------                                     <
 90  >  TOTAL SALES (000'S)                      1420      1467     1519            <
 91  >  TOTAL COSTS (000'S)                      1036      1057     1074            <
 92  >  OVERALL COST %                         .729577  .720518  .707044            <
 93  >  INVENTORY, ENDING(000'S)        945       967       987     1002            <
 94  >  _____             <
```

of the year in order to "gear up" for the increased sales levels in the first and second quarters. It is also assumed that lower-than-normal levels of staffing and expenses are required in off-season periods and that expenses related to selling product B will not be significant compared to those involved with products A and C.

We now enter the unit volume, by product, and the related sales price per unit for the first month on the appropriate Row from 35 through 42 in Column F. The cost-of-goods-sold (COGS) ratios on Rows 37, 40, and 43 in Column F aredetermined by the following formula:

>F37:@IF(F35<11001,.7,@IF(F35<12001,.685,@IF(F35<13001,.675,.67)))

Translation:

> IF (SALES.UNITS) <10001, THEN COGS% = 70
> ELSE IF (SALES.UNITS) <12001, THEN COGS% = 68.5
> ELSE IF (SALES.UNITS) <13001, THEN COGS% = 67.5
> ELSE COGS% = 67

By using this series of "less than" tests, you can relate a given level of sales to a given COGS ratio. If sales are in excess of a given level, the next test will be applied and so on until the appropriate level is reached. In other words, this formula determines the unit level of sales and uses the appropriate cost-of-goods-sold rate for that volume level. The underlying assumption is that as volume increases, materials are purchased in greater quantities to meet the increased production requirements. The higher-volume purchases are assumed, for this example, to result in lower costs per unit purchased. A "lookup" table could have been used in place of the @IF approach in order to achieve the same result (see Chapter 2 for such an example).

Sales volumes for subsequent months are computed using the following formula:

>G35:@INT((F35*@CHOOSE(G18,F28...I28))+.5)

Translation:

SALES.MONTH = (SALES.PREVIOUS * SEASONFACTOR.QUARTER)

We have used the @CHOOSE function to select the season factor for the quarter code shown in G18. Note the use of the @INT function in these formulas. This is used in order to round the results of the calculations to the nearest dollar for purposes of display and also further calculation and should be disregarded when the logic of the cell entry is considered. This technique will also avoid the needless misfootings that result from using a global or local integer display function to round the display itself while retaining the full number in the cell for further computations. We assume that our numbers will all be positive, and therefore we haven't used the more accurate rounding formula described on page 47.

After the unit volume and other data have been entered for all three products, we proceed to the next portion of the data-input area. Here, in Columns B through D, we enter the titles of various expense categories in the operating ratio portion of the template on Rows 48 through 70. In Column E we enter their related basis codes. These codes denote their relationship to sales or other factors such as payroll. The operating ratios relate to income and expense items in the statement of income, also known as the operating statement. They encompass the relationship of the income and expense accounts as well as operating factors such as inventory turnover. These will be used to compute the operating expenses as a percent of income or other factors in the projected statement of income. The basis code is a number which will be used to "lookup" the proper seasonal factor in the seasonal table described above.

There are several basis codes which are neither found in nor related to the seasonal table. These codes, 7 through 10, are used merely as a reference to indicate the different bases used for computing expenses. They may be used by the preparer, reviewer, or another user to rethink the reasonableness of the methods used and the relationship of the various methods used to compute the expense factors. For example, Basis Code 8 is used to indicate that these expenses are computed by totaling all payroll accounts and multiplying the total by an appropriate percent. Anyone could review the items having this code and determine that this basis was, in fact, reasonable in relation to the type of expense being calculated.

Each of these codes is defined by the user and can be used to mean practically anything. However, for the benefit of other possible users of the template, they should be explained somewhere on the template itself or in accompanying written documentation.

Other means of identifying the bases for computations, such as labels, may be used as well. These include the examples for interest expense, which is calculated on the basis of notes outstanding, and income taxes, which are based upon income before income taxes (IBIT). You will note that some of these expense categories contain absolute dollar amounts, while others contain percentages. Our example assumes that certain expenses have known dollar amounts, such as monthly rent, and others, such as commissions, are calculated as a percent of sales.

The financial ratio portion of the input area, Rows 74 through 78, contains various standard financial ratios used in the analysis of financial statements. Financial ratios relate to asset, liability, and equity accounts contained in the balance sheet. They are sometimes used to compare businesses in the same industry. For example, the current ratio—the ratio of current assets to current liabilities—may be relatively constant from company to company within a given industry due to the nature of the industry itself. However, there may be substantial differences in current ratios in one industry compared to another industry.

Financial ratios are useful in reviewing a set of financial statements and learning something about the health of a business. In preparing financial projections, these same ratios can be used, in reverse, to calculate the initial period's balances of various balance sheet accounts. Similarly, the operating ratios are used to obtain the amounts for the first period's statement of income. Amounts for all periods after the first period are computed from the results of the immediately preceding period. For example, sales salaries in January are computed based upon the data in the user input area. Sales salaries for February are then computed by multiplying the previous month's salaries by the seasonal and inflationary factors.

Of course, using these operating and financial ratios assumes that you know something about these historical ratios for your company and that you expect them to remain relatively constant during the projection period. This is impossible when you are preparing projections for a new business in the development stage, since you have no historical figures to use as guidelines. In such a situation you might refer to industry statistics to obtain these data.

The first financial ratio that we use is Inventory Days, on Row 74. This is the average number of days that our inventory remains in stock. Stated another way, this is the number of times per year that our average inventory is sold. The remaining items in this section, Cash Days in Operating Expenses, Accounts Receivable Days, Accounts Payable Days, and Accrued Expense Days, relate to the time required for accounts receivable to be collected and for merchandise purchases and operating expenses to be paid in cash. These ratios will therefore be used to calculate such items as ending accounts receivable and payable balances for balance sheet purposes, and related cash collections and disbursements for the statement of cash flow.

The next input area, Rows 82 through 85, contains miscellaneous data required to properly complete the template. These relate primarily to the projected balance sheets and projected statements of cash flow. The property plant and equipment amounts represent estimated average expenditures on a monthly basis for these needs. If more detail is known, such as the actual months in which these major expenditures will occur, those assumptions may be used in place of averages by placing the amount of the periodic expenditure in the input area and referencing that cell within the body of the report in the appropriate periods. For example, long-term debt repayments based upon loan agreements are assumed to require monthly principal repayments of $3,000.

The last portion of the user input and interim calculations section contains interim calculations on Rows 90 through 93. In this area we have computed total sales, total cost of goods sold, and an overall cost of goods sold percent—that is, total costs divided by total sales. The first two of these computations are made by adding up the mathematical products of the sales and cost-of-sales calculations made above. The formula for sales is

>F90:(@INT(((F35*F36)+(F38*F39)+(F41*F42))/1000)+.5))

Translation:

SALES = (SALES.UNITS.A * PRICE.UNITS.A) +
(SALES.UNITS.B * PRICE.UNITS.B) +
(SALES.UNITS.C * PRICE.UNITS.C)

With the understanding that SALES of a product are equal to SALES.UNITS multiplied by PRICE.UNITS, the formula for cost of goods sold (COGS) is

>F91:(@INT(((F35*F36*F37)+(F38*F39*F40)+(F41*F42*F43)/1000)+.5))

Translation:

COGS.TOTAL = (SALES.A * COGS%.A) + (SALES.B * COGS%.B) + (SALES.C * COGS%.C)

Remember, the COGS ratio developed on Rows 37, 40, and 43 represents the costs at the proper sales volumes for the periods in question.

Although the formulas in the computed fields and the data entered in the "Other Data" portions of the template are straightforward, the use of the data in the operating and financial ratios portion of the user input area may not be so obvious. We'll take a closer look at some of these in order to give you an idea of their meaning and use as we discuss the balance of the template in detail.

The next portion of the template contains the report itself—i.e., the projected statement of income shown in Figure 6.2.

Figure 6.2 contains the formulas necessary to calculate the income and expense items for A & A Products and show them in an income statement format.

Actual figures for the prior year are included in Column E as a basis for comparison as well as a source for certain figures required in current-year calculations. The projected statement of income begins with sales on Row 105. The sales are "brought down" from the interim calculation area above. The figures are obtained by the use of the formula "+Xn", which is the cell coordinate of

6: Designing an Application

FIGURE 6.2: PROJECTED STATEMENT OF INCOME

	A	B	C	D	E	F	G	H	I
95									
96					A & A PRODUCTS, INC.				
97			PROJECTED STATEMENT OF INCOME FOR THE YEAR 1984						
98					(000'S)				
99									
100							1984		
101					ACTUAL	------	------	------	------
102					1983	JAN	FEB	MAR	TOTAL
103					------	------	------	------	------
104									
105		SALES			15550	1420	1467	1519	4406
106					------	------	------	------	------
107		COST OF SALES:							
108			INVENTORY, BEGINNING		875	945	967	987	875
109			PURCHASES		12443	1058	1077	1089	3224
110					------	------	------	------	------
111					13318	2003	2044	2076	6123
112			INVENTORY, ENDING		945	967	987	1002	1002
113					------	------	------	------	------
114		COST OF SALES			12373	1036	1057	1074	3167
115					------	------	------	------	------
116		GROSS PROFIT			3177	384	410	445	1239
117					------	------	------	------	------
118									
119		OPERATING EXPENSES:							
120									
121		SALARIES, OFFICERS			250	24	24	24	72
122		SALARIES, OFFICE			342	30	30	30	90
123		SALARIES, SALES			165	20	21	22	63
124		PAYROLL TAXES			60	6	6	6	18
125		ADVERTISING			131	21	22	24	67
126		BAD DEBT EXPENSE			165	21	22	24	67
127		COMMISSIONS			443	43	46	49	138
128		DELIVERY			187	20	21	22	63
129		DEPRECIATION			76	9	9	9	27
130		GROUP INSURANCE			65	6	6	6	18
131		INSURANCE			67	8	8	8	24
132		INTEREST			87	14	12	11	37
133		LEGAL & ACCOUNTING			46	5	5	5	15
134		MOTOR VEHICLE EXPENSE			41	4	4	4	12
135		OFFICE SUPPLIES & EXPNSE			37	4	4	4	12
136		RENT			48	4	4	4	12
137		REPAIRS & MAINTENANCE			51	5	5	5	15
138		SELLING			106	11	12	13	36
139		TAXES, OTHER			15	2	2	2	6
140		TELEPHONE			30	3	3	3	9
141		TRADE SHOWS			18	4	4	4	12
142		TRAVEL			60	6	6	6	18
143					------	------	------	------	------
144		OPERATING EXPENSES			2490	270	276	285	831
145					------	------	------	------	------
146		INCOME BEFORE INCOME TAX			687	114	134	160	408
147		INCOME TAXES			287	50	59	70	179
148					------	------	------	------	------
149		NET INCOME			400	64	75	90	229
150					======	======	======	======	======

the cell which contains the appropriate number. In this case, sales for January are brought down into Cell F105 from Cell F90:

>F105: +F90

Note that we could have computed sales figures in Cell F105 and eliminated F90 in the interim calculation section. However, we believe that the model is easier to read and understand as written. If the extra memory required for this method were of concern, ease of understanding would have to give way to practicalities of memory usage.

Beginning inventory figures, Row 108, are brought forward from the previous month's ending inventory figure on Row 112 with the formula "+E112". Purchases, Row 109, are calculated by backing into the figure based upon beginning and ending inventories and the known cost-of-goods-sold figure computed on Row 91 above. This is accomplished with the formula:

>F109: +F91+F93−F108

PURCHASES = (COGS.TOTAL + INVENTORY.END − INVENTORY.BEGIN)

The ending inventory, Row 112, is brought down from Row 93 in the interim calculation area above. Cost of sales and gross profit, Rows 114 and 116 respectively, are computed by simple subtraction.

Now we begin the operating expenses. Officers' and sales salaries are brought down from the input area for the first month. Officers' salaries for subsequent months are based upon a formula which includes a management bonus arrangement.

>G121:IF(@AND(E31>1.02,@SUM(F149...F149)>2250,G17<10), @INT(F121*E31^(G17−1))+.5)+100,@INT(F121* (E31^(G17−1))+.5))

IF INFLATION% > 2 AND INCOME.CUM >$2,250,000 AND MONTH < 10)

THEN SALARIES.OFFICERS = SALARIES.OFFICERS.PREVIOUS * INFLATION% COMPOUNDED + $100,000

ELSE SALARIES.OFFICERS = SALARIES.OFFICERS.PREVIOUS * INFLATION% COMPOUNDED.

This formula presumes that officers will receive salary increases in proportion to inflation, even though they will not receive any bonus, and this increase has been computed monthly, although the officers may actually receive cost of living increases annually or semiannually. Note that in subsequent months, @SUM(F149...F149) changes to @SUM(F149...G149), @SUM(F149...H149) and so on. The increment in the second reference is needed in order to obtain the cumulative net income to date.

Note also that the exponent factor used for compounding is the number of the current month less 1, as the first month itself is the base period and is not compounded. This exponential method is necessary in order to compound the inflation factor properly, since we have used the built-in @INT function to round the results of each month's formula. If we did not use the exponential method, the result in any particular month would be rounded to the nearest thousand dollars, and the portion dropped off or added onto the result would have an unwanted effect on the results of future months. However, using the exponential function combined with the @INT function, you can achieve both goals, rounding the monthly display and cell contents and compounding the amounts correctly.

Sales salaries are increased monthly by the rate of inflation and the seasonality factors. The formula is

>G123:(@INT((F123*E31*@IF(E50=1,@CHOOSE(G18,F25...I25),
@IF(E50=2,@CHOOSE(G18,F26...I26),
@CHOOSE(G18,F27...I27))))+.5))

Translation:

**SALARIES.SALES = SALARIES.SALES.PREVIOUS * INFLATION%
*SEASONFACTOR.QUARTER**

where the seasonal factors are selected with a combination of the @IF and @CHOOSE statements such that

**IF BASIS = 1, THEN CHOOSE SEASONFACTOR.PAYROLL
ELSE IF BASIS = 2, THEN CHOOSE SEASONFACTOR.SALES
ELSE IF BASIS = 3, THEN CHOOSE SEASONFACTOR.OTHER**

(You did remember that Row 25, Row 26, and Row 27 related to payroll basis, sales basis, or "other" basis, didn't you?)

Office salaries are computed based upon the compounded inflation rate itself. Again the compounding is performed by a formula which contains a cell reference to the inflation rate rather than the numeric inflation rate itself. In this manner we may utilize the same inflation rate throughout various formulas in the model. When we wish to change the rate of inflation, we only need to alter the one coordinate containing the rate, which is referred to by the various formulas. This use of variables is a great time-saver and will allow you to construct models for a much wider range of applications.

Payroll taxes, as well as group insurance below, are computed as percentages of total payroll. Note that no consideration has been given to the effect that payroll per employee in excess of maximum limits would have on overall payroll taxes. In other words, this model does not provide for situations where one or more employees reached the maximum limit for social security (FICA) deductions and so these payroll taxes were no longer proportionate to payroll. You know from experience that your banker will not require you to be that exact. If you wish to be that exact, you may alter the model to provide the number of employees at various salary levels and use these data to compute payroll.

Rows 125 through 128—advertising, bad debt expense, commissions, and delivery—are based upon a percentage of sales, typified by the formula:

>F125:(@INT((+F52*F105)+.5))

Subsequent months' figures are first inflated by the monthly inflation rate, then multiplied by the seasonality factor applicable to that type of expense, as defined by the basis code associated with that item in the input section above.

Depreciation on Row 129 is brought down from the input area. However, it could have been calculated within the model, based upon the beginning balance in the property and equipment account and the estimated acquisitions during the projection period.

Group insurance, Row 130, is a percent of total payroll above, while general insurance, Row 131, is brought down from the designated amount in the input area. In subsequent months general insurance is inflated and seasonally adjusted as explained above. The seasonal adjustment assumes that these costs will vary with the activity level of sales since product liability and other types of insurance may increase. For the accrual basis statement of income, these costs, if significant, could be adjusted monthly.

Interest expense, Row 132, is computed each month by taking one twelfth of the annual interest rate in Cell F59 and multiplying it by the outstanding indebtedness at the end of the previous month.

>F132:(@INT((F59/12*E235)+.5))

This calculates interest on last month's ending balance. We expect to have a fairly constant borrowing. If your outstanding loan balance were to fluctuate greatly from month to month, you might want to calculate interest on the current period's balance in order to match the interest charges more directly with the time you held the funds. Although this would be more technically correct from an accounting viewpoint, it would cause forward references.

Expenses for legal and accounting fees, Row 133, through repairs and maintenance, Row 137; taxes, other, Row 139; and telephone expenses, Row 140, are all based upon the monthly amounts brought down from the input area and then compounded in future months by the inflation rate and seasonal factors. Selling expense, Row 138; trade shows, Row 141; and travel, Row 142, are all based upon a percent of sales in the first month and are compounded by the inflation rate and seasonal factors in future months.

All of the operating expenses are then totaled, using the SUM function—e.g., @SUM(E121...E143)—and are then subtracted from gross profit to arrive at income before income taxes. Note that the model does not assume any "other" income or expenses, nor are there any extraordinary items. Should your situation call for such items, they can easily be built in to the model or added later. In addition, note that interest expense has been included with operating expenses in order to simplify the model. However, in most situations it might be included as an item of "other expense." The row containing the underline (------), Row 143, has intentionally been included in the @SUM formula to allow for possible later insertion of a row (or rows) after unclassified expenses.

Income taxes, on Row 147, are computed as a percentage of net income before income taxes, Row 146. In this case, a flat rate of 44 percent, as shown in Cell F70, is used. This is assumed to be the average federal and state combined rate, taking into consideration the first $100,000 of income, which is taxed at substantially lower federal rates; state rates, which may be graduated; and taxes which may be reduced by investment and other credits. Again, if you wish to be exact, you may use a formula that will apply different rates to various layers of income and then reduce the taxes by a percent of the equipment additions representing investment and other credits.

The third portion of the template includes another interim calculation and user input area, as shown in Figure 6.3.

This input area is separated from the previous input/calculation area since many of these items are dependent upon the results of the calculations contained in the projected statements of income. The user must take care in entering data in these areas so that formulas relating to the interim calculations required in this portion of the template are not accidentally overwritten. A simple way to avoid such problems is to use "label" entries in those cells requiring user input. The labels—e.g., "<AMOUNT>" and "<RATIO>"—may be used to describe the type of input required.

This area contains additional user input consisting of prepaid items, other assets, and common stock. These interim calculations are necessary in order to complete the projected balance sheets and the projected statements of cash flow. Although these items could have been computed directly within the respective statements, forward references would have been required, necessitating multiple recalculations in order to obtain the proper results in the model.

Income taxes paid are based upon one fourth of the total estimated tax due for the coming year. This estimate can be the amount necessary under IRS regulations to avoid a penalty for underestimation of taxes, or it may be another appropriate amount. In the model, one-fourth of the total estimated taxes, based upon 100 percent of the prior year's taxes, is shown as payment in the proper month in which it is due, based upon IRS regulations. This formula checks the month in

FIGURE 6.3: SECOND USER INPUT AREA

	A	B	C	D	E	F	G	H	I
151									
152		>>>>>>>>>>>>>>>>>>>>			USER	INPUT	<<<<<<<<<<<<<<<<<<<<		
153		>			AND				<
154		>	INTERIM		CALCULATIONS				<
155		>							<
156		>					1984		<
157		>			1983	----------------------			<
158		>			ACTUAL	JAN.	FEB.	MAR.	<
159		>			------	------	------	------	<
160		> INCOME TAXES PAID			0	0	0	40	<
161		> CASH REQUIRED			321	522	534	512	<
162		> ACCOUNTS RECEIVABLE			2167	2130	2201	2278	<
163		> INVENTORY			945	967	987	1002	<
164		> PREPAID ITEMS	<INPUT>		132	132	132	132	<
165		> PROPERTY, PLANT & EQUIP.			437	438	439	440	<
166		> OTHER ASSETS	<INPUT>		76	76	76	76	<
167		> TOTAL ASSETS			4078	4265	4369	4440	<
168		> COMMON STOCK	<INPUT>		300	300	300	300	<
169		> RETAINED EARNINGS			1259	1323	1398	1488	<
170		> LONG TERM DEBT			180	177	174	171	<
171		> TOTAL CURRENT LIABS.			2339	2465	2497	2481	<
172		> ACCOUNTS PAYABLE			943	1234	1257	1271	<
173		> ACCRUED EXPENSES			256	187	192	200	<
174		> INCOME TAXES PAYABLE			40	90	149	179	<
175		> NOTES PAYABLE			1100	954	899	831	<
176		>							<

which the calculation is being made and then completes the calculation only in the appropriate months. The formula is

>F160:@IF(@OR(F17=4,F17=6,F17=9,F17=12),@INT((E147/4+.5), @IF(F17= 3,+E237,0)))

Translation:

IF MONTH = (APRIL OR JUNE OR SEPTEMBER OR DECEMBER)
  THEN TAX.PAYMENT = TAX.ESTIMATE.YEAR / 4
    ELSE = MONTH = MARCH, THEN TAX.PAYMENT = TAX.DUE.LY ELSE 0.

Cash required, Row 161, begins with total expenses shown in the statement of income for the current month, less noncash expenses. Our only noncash expense here is depreciation. However, the expenses are presented on an accrual basis, i.e., as incurred, rather than on a cash basis when they are paid. A formula is required to convert these expenses from the accrual to the cash basis. The formula computes the daily expenses and uses the number of days that operating expenses are historically carried until payment is made to convert the monthly total to a cash basis. The formula is:

>F161:(@INT((F144−F129)/30*F75)+.5)

Translation:

CASH.REQ = (EXPENSES.TOTAL − DEPRECIATION) / 30 * DAYS.OPERATING.EXPENSES

The result is the cash required to pay the expenses in the current month.

Similarly, accounts receivable are converted to cash on a monthly basis, thereby providing cash with which to pay expenses and make debt repayments. The accounts receivable formula calculates the ending balance of accounts receivable based upon historical information relative to collection periods. In this case, our computation is based upon the number of days' sales included in accounts receivable. Knowing last month's ending accounts receivable balance, this month's ending balance, and the sales for the period, we can calculate the accounts receivable collected during the current period by difference. The ending accounts receivable is calculated by the following formula:

>F162:(@INT((F105/30*F76)+.5))

RECEIVABLES=(SALES.PREVIOUS/30*)DAYS.RECEIVABLES

Ending inventory is brought down from above merely as an aid in reviewing and following the logic of the template. Where space and/or memory is a vital consideration, this interim item could be deleted, and ending inventory in the statement of income would be pulled directly into the month-end balance sheet.

Prepaid items may include prepaid expenses, security deposits, and similar items, which remain relatively constant. Therefore, the amounts may be given here as absolute values rather than figures to be derived through formulas. The same is true for other assets and common stock, which are also reflected as designated amounts.

The item property, plant, and equipment is calculated by taking the balance at the beginning of the month, plus additions in the current month, less depreciation for the current month. The formula is

$$>F165: +E224+F82-F129$$

Other asset amounts are given as absolute values. The total asset computation is made here in order to provide the amount necessary when calculating debt balances needed to balance the projected balance sheets. Again, this allows for the proper computation of ending debt balances without the necessity for forward references.

Retained earnings and long-term debt are calculated as the sum of the previous period's balances plus the current period's activities. Computing these balances at this time also allows us to calculate total current liabilities, which will be required in order to compute, or back into, notes payable below. Remember, some amounts required for the projected financial statements may need to be calculated prior to other amounts that are necessary for other parts of the statements. Thus the necessity for these interim calculations.

The items to be included in current liabilities are now calculated individually. Although there is nothing magic about these computations, they must be made here rather than in the projected balance sheets themselves in order to compute the final current liability figure—notes payable—which is a result, in effect, of the cash requirements of the business. The figure for accounts payable is calculated by multiplying the average day's purchases times the number of days purchases normally go unpaid, i.e., the amount included in ending accounts payable. The formula is

$$>F172:(@INT((F109/30*F77)+.5))$$

Similarly, accrued expenses are calculated as total operating expenses less salaries and depreciation converted to a daily average and then multiplied by the number of days that accrued expenses are normally outstanding. Taxes payable are calculated by adding the unpaid balance at the end of the previous period and the tax on the income for the current month and then subtracting the amount paid during the current month. It is now possible to determine the required ending balance of notes payable in order to balance the projected balance sheets. This operation will provide the information necessary to compute the increase or decrease in notes payable, which in turn will enable you to calculate the cash flow relative to notes payable in the projected statements of cash flow.

The remaining task is simple. We only need to bring the amounts already computed into the projected statements of cash flow and the projected balance sheets. In several instances, we will perform some additional calculations within these statements to arrive at the appropriate balances. However, these will be

FIGURE 6.4: PROJECTED STATEMENTS OF CASH FLOW

A	B	C	D	E	F	G	H
177							
178			A & A PRODUCTS, INC.				
179		PROJECTED CASH FLOW FOR THE YEAR 1984					
180			(000'S)				
181							
182					JAN	FEB	MAR
183					------	------	------
184	RECEIPTS:						
185	CASH, BEGINNING				321	522	534
186	A/R COLLECTIONS				1457	1396	1442
187	NOTE ADDITIONS				0	0	0
188	LONG TERM DEBT				0	0	0
189					------	------	------
190		TOTAL AVAILABLE CASH			1778	1918	1976
191					------	------	------
192	DISBURSEMENTS:						
193	PROPERTY, PLANT & EQUIP.				10	10	10
194	ACCOUNTS PAYABLE				767	1054	1075
195	ACCRUED EXPENSES				330	262	268
196	NOTE REPAYMENTS				146	55	68
197	LONG TERM DEBT				3	3	3
198	INCOME TAXES				0	0	40
199					------	------	------
200		TOTAL CASH DISBURSED			1256	1384	1464
201					------	------	------
202	CASH, ENDING				522	534	512
203					======	======	======
204							

minimal and will involve simple addition and subtraction. These include the calculations of accounts receivable collections, payments of accounts payable, accrued expenses, and notes payable. The formulas for the balance of the projection period in the projected statements of income, projected balance sheets and projected statements of cash flow are replicated from the formulas for the first or second month of the projection period, as appropriate.

The last area of the template contains the projected statements of cash flow, Figure 6.4, and the projected balance sheets, Figure 6.5. These statements result from the formulas contained within the reports and from the interim calculations and user input contained in the above portions of the template. The amounts are either brought down from figures derived above or are the result of simple additions and subtractions.

Now that the template is complete, you can point out best case and worst case versions for your banker, permitting approval of your loan before he or she goes on vacation. (You may even wish to print out a third projection—what you think will really happen.) But don't throw the template away. As you proceed from month to month in your expanded operation, you may replace the monthly figures with the actual figures for those periods to obtain better estimates for the balance of the year. This presumes, of course, that you still accept the validity of the original formulas (assumptions) used to project income, expenses, assets, liabilities and equity. If the actual figures for several months lead you to believe that your original assumptions were incorrect, you may change the appropriate formula(s) for the balance of the projection period.

We do not expect that you will be able to use the template discussed in this chapter exactly as written. We do hope, however, that the template design and our explanation of the logic used will allow you to use much of it in your work.

FIGURE 6.5: PROJECTED BALANCE SHEETS

```
                    A & A PRODUCTS, INC.
            PROJECTED BALANCE SHEETS FOR THE YEAR 1984
                         (000'S)

                                          1984
                              ACTUAL  ---------------------
                               1983    JAN    FEB    MAR
                              ------  ------ ------ ------

                              ASSETS

  CURRENT ASSETS:
    CASH                        321     522    534    512
    ACCOUNTS RECEIVABLE        2167    2130   2201   2278
    INVENTORY                   945     967    987   1002
    PREPAID ITEMS               132     132    132    132
                              ------  ------ ------ ------
  TOTAL CURRENT ASSETS         3565    3751   3854   3924

  PROPERTY, PLANT & EQUIP.      437     438    439    440

  OTHER ASSETS                   76      76     76     76
                              ------  ------ ------ ------
  TOTAL ASSETS                 4078    4265   4369   4440
                              ======  ====== ====== ======

          LIABILITIES AND SHAREHOLDERS' EQUITY

  CURRENT LIABILITIES:
    NOTES PAYABLE              1100     954    899    831
    ACCOUNTS PAYABLE            943    1234   1257   1271
    ACCRUED EXPENSES            256     187    192    200
    INCOME TAXES                 40      90    149    179
                              ------  ------ ------ ------
  TOTAL CURRENT
      LIABILITIES              2339    2465   2497   2481
                              ------  ------ ------ ------
  LONG TERM DEBT                180     177    174    171
                              ------  ------ ------ ------
  SHAREHOLDERS' EQUITY:
    COMMON STOCK                300     300    300    300
    RETAINED EARNINGS          1259    1323   1398   1488
                              ------  ------ ------ ------
  TOTAL EQUITY                 1559    1623   1698   1788
                              ------  ------ ------ ------
  TOTAL LIABILITIES AND
      SHAREHOLDERS' EQUITY     4078    4265   4369   4440
                              ======  ====== ====== ======
  DOWNFOOT PROOF                  0       0      0      0
```

PART IV

VisiCalc—The Advanced Version

INTRODUCTION

The first version, or "stage," of VisiCalc, originally available for the 13 Sector Apple II, had the format and "feel" of VisiCalc as we know it today, but it lacked such Boolean features as @IF and the ability to save and load files in the Data Interchange Format (DIF). Second-stage VisiCalc (versions 193 and later for the Apple II, and all versions for the Apple /// and the IBM PC) added, among other things, Boolean features, DIF, and the ability to edit entries in a cell.

In early autumn, 1982, VisiCorp began shipping a third-stage VisiCalc, known as the Advanced Version, or VCAV for short. The first VCAV was for the Apple ///. In 1982, owners of the old Apple /// version of VisiCalc could upgrade to VCAV for a $200 charge. As of this writing, VisiCorp has announced that VCAV will be available for the Apple //e and the IBM PC. We can only speculate that versions for new Apple products, if not for the Apple II family of computers, may also appear.

VCAV is a third-generation spreadsheet program, with all of the second-stage capabilities, plus a number of new built-in arithmetic and Boolean functions; date and time arithmetic; keystroke memory, which can be used to create a series of special function keys for shorthand keyboard input ("keyboard macros"); extensive "help" screens; special formatting for report printing; and new global and local format codes, known as attributes. As VCAV is very new, it has not been possible to integrate the discussion of VCAV into the body of this book, nor is it possible to do more than highlight the new features of VCAV and how they can best be used.

One obvious difference between VCAV and second-stage VisiCalc is that VCAV requires the program disk to remain in the built-in disk drive. However, if you have VCAV on a hard disk, such as the Apple Computer, Inc., Profile, you need not keep the floppy disk in its drive. When a command or function is used for the first time in a work session, you may note that a disk read is necessary to get the command or function into the computer. If you call for the same function or command immediately thereafter, a disk read would not be required. If you don't use that command or function for a while, however, it can get pushed out of memory, and it may be necessary to reread it from disk the next time you use it. For that reason, VCAV might not seem to work quite as fast as you are accustomed to, but the new features in VCAV are well worth any slight delay.

CHAPTER 7

New Features

This chapter contains a description of the new features of VCAV. In addition, selected tips and warnings are included with the description of each feature, to help you in beginning to learn about VCAV.

THE FINANCIAL FUNCTIONS

VCAV adds a complete series of built-in functions to automatically perform financial calculations relating to equal-payment loan-amortization models. With the new built-in functions, one can calculate the interest rate using @RATE, the number of payments to be made using @PERIODS, the amount of each periodic payment using @PMT, and the present and future values using @PV (present value) and @FV, respectively. Each of these built-in functions calculates the indicated figure, given any three of the four others.

For example, if one knows the periodic interest rate, the number of equal periodic payments, and the loan amount (the "present value"), the amount of the periodic payment required to amortize the loan can be calculated directly by the formula

@PMT(rate, number of payments, − (present value), @NA).

Note that "present value" must be entered as the negative of the actual amount of the loan (or converted to the negative in the cell reference). The @NA in this example is where the future value would normally appear, but as long as we have three pieces of data, the fourth value is not needed except as a formula placeholder.

If we know that the interest rate is 9.75 percent, on a 29-year mortgage (payable monthly), for an initial principal balance of $70,000, the formula

@PMT(.0975/12,348, −70000,@NA)

will yield the result $604.95 if rounded to the nearest penny. Further, if B2 contains the loan's percent as a whole number, B4 the number of years, and B6 the amount of the loan,

>B10:@PMT(B2/1200,B4*12, −(B6),@NA)

will calculate the appropriate payment.

In these examples, @NA is used to represent the "future value" of the cash flow, which is often not known in such situations. If, however, we know only the interest rate, a projected required college tuition, and the date a child will be ready for college, we can calculate the tuition that will be required when the child attains college age, using the formula

@PMT(rate, number of payments, @NA, tuition)

Once again, as long as three of the four values are known, the fourth may be represented by the @NA function. The values in an @PMT function must always be presented in this order: rate, number of payments, present value, and future value. Of course each value may be represented by a cell reference rather than a directly entered number. Finally, rate must be entered as, or converted to, a decimal fraction and must match the assumed frequency of payments. That is, if the interest rate is 14.5 percent, and one wishes to calculate on the basis of monthly payments, the 14.5 percent entry must be converted to a monthly basis (14.5/1200).

If a cell reference is used to permit entry of rate in a separate cell, a new VisiCalc feature, the "%" command may be used to convert 14.5 to .145, and the @PMT entry need only divide the cell reference by 12. The "%" command (not to be confused with the % attribute) works like the "#" command. Simply move the cursor to the cell with the number you wish to change from a decimal fraction to a percent, enter "%", hit **[RETURN],** and the number in the cell is automatically divided by 100.

Similarly, one could solve for the rate of interest. The formula

>B10:(@RATE(B2*12,B4, −(B6),@NA)*12)

will calculate the interest rate, where the term of the loan in years is in B2, the amount of the monthly payment is in B4, and the principal amount is in B6. Note that @RATE has its own required variable order, which must be respected.

@IRR calculates a cash flow's internal rate of return using the syntax

@IRR (present value, begin range...end range)

Thus, the formula

>B10:@IRR(A1,A2...A11)

will calculate an internal rate of return of the cash flow listed in the range A2 to A11, based upon the investment shown in Cell A1.

Taken together, these built-in financial functions add the capability of a moderately priced electronic business calculator to VisiCalc, enabling the program to do directly what could previously be done only indirectly. The financial functions are easy to use and are a welcome addition.

THE ARITHMETIC FUNCTIONS

Three new arithmetic functions are present: @ROUND, @DOTPROD, and @MOD. @ROUND uses the syntax

@ROUND *(expression, n)*

where *expression* is the value to be rounded. According to the latest VCAV manual we have seen, *n* is an integer from −59 to +59, representing the number of decimal places to the left (for negative values) or right (for positive values) of the decimal point that you wish to round to. "0" will round *expression* to the nearest integer. A (−3) will round expression to the nearest thousand. @ROUND(12353556,−3), for example, will return 12354000. As we are told in the VCAV manual that VisiCalc stores its numbers to 11 or possibly 12 significant digits, the meaning of rounding that number to 59—or even 30—digits from the decimal point is not at all clear. Perhaps the range of −59 to +59 presages a quintuple-precision version of VisiCalculations, that is, a version of VisiCalc that will be accurate to 60 digits. At the moment, however, it would appear that −11 to +11 is probably the greatest usable range.

@ROUND differs from formatting ("/FI" or "/F$") in that @ROUND actually rounds the calculation value of expression rather than just rounding the cell display as is done by the formatting commands. @ROUND eliminates the need for the rounding formula discussed in Chapter 4. Once again, you can do it with second-stage VisiCalc, but @ROUND is so much easier than the @INT formula.

@DOTPROD calculates the sum of the products of the multiplications of corresponding values in two ranges. This may be useful, for example, for totaling extensions of quantities and unit prices, calculating weighted averages, and similar functions. The syntax is

@DOTPROD(begin1.end1,begin2.end2)

In Figure 7.1 we use the following

>B10:@DOTPROD(A2...A8,B2...B8)

Note that the two ranges used by @DOTPROD need not be adjacent—as required, for example, by @LOOKUP. To illustrate the power of @DOTPROD, the B10 formula shown above is the equivalent of

((A2*B2)+(A3*B3)+(A4*B4)+(A5*B5)+(A6*B6)+(A7*B7)+(A8*B8))

FIGURE 7.1

	A	B
1	# OF UNITS	$ PER UNIT
2	13	100.92
3	12	.48
4	1	10.15
5	145	.99
6	2	.09
7	23	13.01
8	11	9.92
9		---------
10	TOTAL COST:	1879.95

or, to use more familiar VisiCalc shorthand,

@SUM(A2*B2,A3*B3,A4*B4,A5*B5,A6*B6,A7*B7,A8*B8)

If the individual products (A2*B2) have already been calculated and placed into a third column (C2, for example), a simple @SUM will do the job. @DOTPROD is useful where it is not desired to know the value of each individual line, and only the total is required.

@MOD calculates the remainder resulting when one number is divided by another. @MOD(10,8) is equal to 2, while @MOD(8,8) is equal to 0. @MOD will be most useful in esoteric algebraic manipulations but will also come in handy if you wish to determine whether the numbered month in question is the beginning of the quarter. Assuming that the number of the month (from 1 to 12) is placed in D20, the formula @MOD(D20,3) will equal "1" in January, April, July, and October. This can be compared to the method used in THE template (see Chapter 6) with second-stage VisiCalc.

RETURNING LABELS WITH THE LOOKUP FUNCTIONS

One of the weaknesses of second-stage VisiCalc is that the lookup functions @CHOOSE and @LOOKUP are able to return only numbers. Teachers wishing to assign A's or F's within specific grade ranges automatically, and stock analysts wishing to generate "BUY" or "SELL" messages, had to settle for awkward half measures. The new functions @LCHOOSE, @LABEL, and @VALUE enable the user to accomplish these long-sought-after miracles.

@LCHOOSE works just like @CHOOSE (see Appendix A) except that the function will return the contents of a cell (even if the contents consist of a label) rather than merely its value. Thus if "A" is in A1, "B" is in B1, and "C" is in C1,

@LCHOOSE(3,A1,B1,C1)

will return the letter C.

If a student's grade point average is represented in Cell A1, and the labels "F", "D", "C", "B", and "A" are placed into Cells A5 through A9, respectively,

>C20:@LCHOOSE (@INT(A1)+1,A5,A6,A7,A8,A9)

or

>C20:@LCHOOSE (A1,A5...A9)

will place the appropriate letter grade into Cell C20.

As another example, @LABEL*(expression)* will display the contents, including displaying a label, of any referenced cell returned by *expression*. @LABEL permits the user to obtain the same "returned labels" with functions such as @LOOKUP, as with @LCHOOSE. In fact, @LABEL(@CHOOSE*(expression)* is equivalent to @LCHOOSE*(expression)*. Using the same values as shown in the preceding paragraph, the same "A", "B", "C", "D", "F" result can be achieved with the function

>C20:@LABEL(@CHOOSE(A1,A5...A9))

Even better, @LCHOOSE(A1,A5...A9) will return a blank if A1 is equal to 1, and A5 is a blank cell. This is just the thing for those tables where you have previously settled for answers of "0" or "@NA" but where you really wanted a plain empty cell.

The VCAV manual warns that a returned label (using @LABEL or @LCHOOSE) is treated as a "value" for @COUNT, @AVERAGE, @MIN, and @MAX purposes. When the user wishes to make certain that a true value is returned by one of these "counting" functions, the new function @VALUE should be used.

All of this is rather confusing to read about, but after some time using VCAV, @VALUE will become old hat. The ability to return labels rather than values with the lookup functions makes for much nicer looking reports and displays and is a very welcome addition, if for no other reason than your reports can now answer JANUARY and APRIL, rather than fudging with months equal to 1 or 4.

DATE ARITHMETIC

With the new functions @MDY, @VMDY, and @HMS, VCAV can automatically convert from an inputted time and date to the number of days (and hours, minutes, and seconds) between that moment and the first instant of January 1, 1979 (a date chosen arbitrarily but used uniformly). @YEAR, @MONTH, @DAY, @HOURS, @MINUTES, and @SECONDS enable the VCAV user to convert from a numeric value to its equivalent date. These functions make it possible to compare dates to determine the age of a person or an account, the yield to maturity of a bond, or the number of hours that a professional has worked on a project. As is usually the case, cell references may be used with the date functions, so that months, days, and years may be entered into adjoining cells.

For example, January 1, 1980, could be represented as 1,1,1980. @MDY(1,1,1980) is equal to 365, and @MDY(1,1,1978) is equal to −365. (Remember that January 1, 1979, is equal to "0", rather than "1".) The formula

>B10:(@MDY(1,1,1980) − @MDY(1,1,1978))

would return the number 730. Using TAB attributes and reducing column widths to three for months and days, and five for years, quite acceptable data-entry and display formats are possible, making it easy to manipulate the dates in question.

@MDY will take an "impossible" set of calendar figures and try to make sense of them. @MDY(14,−3,1982) for example will be understood as a date that is three days less than 14 months after 1,1,1982 (or January 28, 1983). @VMDY is like @MDY, but demands months and days which make sense according to our standard calendars. @VMDY(14,−3,1982) would return only ERROR. @MDY will accept arguments outside of the normal calendar, and does its best to convert an argument to one that makes sense. A 16 in the month column, for example, will be treated the same as a 4 (April) of the following year. @VMDY is just like @MDY except that it will treat a month equal to 16 as an error, and return ERROR.

As another example,

>D3:D1*(D2/36500)*(@VMDY(A2,B2,C2) − @VMDY(A1,B1,C1))

will calculate the simple interest earned on the amount in Cell D1, at an annual interest rate listed in Cell D2 when deposited at the dates listed in Cells A1, B1, and C1 and withdrawn at the dates listed in Cells A2, B2, C2. In other words, this formula figures the interest earned on the number of days between Row 1 and Row 2, on the amount in D1, at an annual interest rate (shown as a percent) in Cell D2.

Similarly, if Column A, Column B, and Column C (starting at Row 10) contain the month, day, and year of origin of a series of accounts, and the date of the report is listed in A5, B5, and C5, the accounts can be aged by replicating the formula

>F10:@INT((@MDY(A5,B5,C5) − @MDY(A10,B10,C10))/30)*30

Cell F10 will then note whether the account is 30, 60, 90, or more days old as of the date of the report. In fact, the formula

>F10:@IF(@INT((@MDY(A5,B5,C5) − @MDY(A10,B10,C10))/30)*30 = F8),(E10),@LABEL(A1))

will show an aged list of receivables when the formula is replicated down Column F (answer NNNRRRNRN), and then the entire Column F range is replicated to Columns G and H (answer NNNNNNRNN as you replicate across). Columns

F, G, and H will list only the receivables that are in the appropriate aging categories. The @LABEL reference to Cell A1, by the way, returns an empty cell, as we have discussed above.

Additional "date arithmetic" functions include @YEAR, @MONTH, and @DAY, which return the appropriate year, month, or day of the numeric argument, relative to the base date of January 1, 1979. @YEAR(−57), for example, is equal to 1978, because the year of that date, which is 57 days prior to January 1, 1979, is 1978. @MONTH(−57) is equal to 11 (November—the month containing the day that is 57 days prior to the base date), and @DAY(−57) is 5.

But VCAV doesn't stop with date arithmetic. It also includes time arithmetic with the addition of the function @HMS, which accepts entries of hours, minutes, and seconds and converts them to a fraction of a day (@HMS(12,0,0) is equal to .5, for example); and @HOUR, @MINUTE, and @SECOND, which will convert a number back to the appropriate hour, minute, or second of the day, respectively. No doubt these functions will be used to deal with everything from scientific experiments, conversion from degrees to radians, and lawyer and accountant billings.

CHAPTER 8

Attributes

Experienced VisiCalc users will boot VCAV, hit the [/] key to review the command line, and note the addition of "A", which stands for attribute. An attribute controls the way the contents of a cell are displayed, and it is similar to a format. But you can mix and match attributes, using several for a given cell, and you can even combine attributes with formats. An attribute will override a conflicting format.

In general, as with formats, attributes affect cell display only and do not affect the number retained in the cell to be used for calculations. As with formats, attributes may affect a single cell, if entered with a "/A" command, or the entire template, if entered with a "/GA" command. As one might expect, local attributes will override global attributes where conflicts exist, and an erasure of a local attribute will return a cell to the globally set attribute. Attributes are saved with a template and are available when you load the template into memory.

Multiple attributes can be used within a single cell. Unless there is direct conflict, each attribute will be effective. Unlike formats, attributes may be replicated into cells already containing data without destroying the data.

When "/A" or "/GA" is entered, the following prompt line appears:

E,H,M,T,L,V,D

This line translates to *expression, hide, mode, tab, label, value,* and *default*. With most of these options, choosing a letter will alter the prompt line to display the selected option together with the characters "Y N D". "Y" stands for "yes" and tells VCAV to establish the selected attribute in the indicated cell. "N", of course, is "no," telling VCAV to turn off the attribute. "D" commands VCAV to return the cell to the default condition which has been globally set for the given attribute.

With all of this in mind, let us get to the attributes themselves.

/AE OR /GAE EXPRESSION

The *expression* attribute displays the left-justified portion of the formula in a cell, rather than the value of the formula. If the cell width is not enough to display the entire formula, the right portion is dropped from the cell display. "/AEY" will not alter a cell which contains a label.

The *global expression* attribute ("/GAEY") is useful in template debugging, during the design phase of your work, but it will probably not be used once the template design is fixed. As we will discuss later, a different width may be set for each column, to make it easier to see longer formulas.

/AH OR /GAH HIDE

"H" is for *hide*, and the "/AHY" attribute does just that, making a cell appear to be blank. This is a very convenient thing to do with areas of the template that contain fixed variables, intermediate calculations, lookup tables, and the like. Since these items should be of no concern to the template user, they can be made literally "transparent." If hidden cells are all bunched into the same columns, and no information which must be displayed is placed into these columns, the existence of these cells can be made even less obvious by setting the individual column widths to "1" using the "/GCC1" command.

It should be noted that a hidden cell is rather vulnerable, and a user could easily and unwittingly overwrite a hidden cell thinking it to be empty. We strongly suggest that cells which are hidden should also be protected using the *mode* attribute described below. It certainly would have been helpful if VCAV had done this automatically, leaving it to the template designer to unprotect the hidden cell if he wishes to do so.

/AM OR /GAM MODE

The *mode* attribute comes complete with its own submenu, and it allows the designer to control whether, and what kind of, data may be entered into a cell. The submenu displayed after entry of the "/AM" command is not the standard "Y N D", but

MODE: P U A L V # D!

which stands for protect, unprotect, all data types, labels, values, numbers, default, and immediate mode.

Protect and Unprotect

"P" and "U" work in tandem, to protect a cell, making it impossible to enter any information at all into the cell, and to return it to normal by unprotecting it.

As suggested before, the "P" option should be used whenever a cell is "hidden." "P" does not prevent the value contained in a cell from being changed if the cells referenced in a protected cell change. Thus, if (+A5) is entered into Cell A6, and A6 is then protected, any change to Cell A5 will change the value of A6. The same thing will occur if a change is made in a formula in another location that replicates into Cell A6. However the formula in A6 cannot be directly altered until the cell is unprotected. The protect option prohibits changing only what has been entered directly into the cell. Another warning is in order here. Protecting a cell will prevent you or another user from inadvertantly destroying data by typing over a cell accidentally. However, if you replicate a source range into a target range which contains protected cells, the protected cells in the target range will be overwritten by the data contained within the cells of the source range. Very unfortunate indeed. If VCAV is to be made truly user proof, it should provide some method of locking out the ability to do anything but enter data within specified data-entry cells.

The Other Modes

"A" permits all data types to be entered into a cell. This is the VisiCalc default mode.

"L" permits only labels to be entered into a cell. Values of any type cannot be entered once "/AML" is chosen.

"V" will permit only values to be entered into a cell. *Values* include formulas, numbers, and cell references.

"#" permits only number entries. Formulas and labels cannot be entered.

"D" returns the cell to the default mode last set with the global mode command, or the default settings in effect upon boot of VCAV.

MAKING YOUR TEMPLATE USER FRIENDLY

Mode attributes can profitably be combined with the "hidden" attribute for user data entry. If the user is expected to enter a name in a cell, "/AML" is the appropriate setting. Entries of dollar or numeric amounts should be set to "/AM#". We cannot think of many cases where the user would or should be expected to enter a formula. But if the occasion arises, the "V" option should be chosen. And, once again, all hidden cells, and even unhidden cells containing items which must not be changed by the user, should be protected, which is quite possibly the most useful of all the mode attributes.

/AT TABS

The *tab* attribute allows a user to automatically proceed from cell to cell as data entries are required. Hitting the **[TAB]** key will place the cursor on the next cell (in row or column order) which has the "/AT" attribute. **[CONTROL-B]** will return the cursor to the previous cell containing a *tab* attribute. Judicious use of "/AT" will make data entry a lot easier for the user.

/AL LABELS WITH GUTTERS

The normal attribute submenu is not used with "/AL".

LABEL: < > L R F C D!

is used instead. This submenu looks much like a standard VisiCalc format menu, but it controls labels only.

"<" left justifies and ">" right justifies a value between "gutters." The "gutter"—or margin between the absolute edge of a cell and where printing is designated to begin or end—is set by "L" on the left edge and "R" on the right. Integer values are required, with "0" (no gutters) as the default value.

"F" is similar to the "/−" command, repeating a label across a cell, but only between the gutters. This attribute will make much neater looking "total" lines if you set a left gutter of one space.

"C" centers a label in a cell, between the gutters specified by "L" and "R".

"D" returns the "/AL" attribute to the current global default.

"!", again is the immediate mode.

/AV VALUES

"/AV" comes with its own submenu, eschewing the standard attribute "Y N D", and it controls the manner in which values are displayed. "/AV" is most directly analogous to a format command, and the submenu is quite a mouthful:

VALUE: < > L R + − (C,.Z % $ G F I S * D

Displaying Values

"<", ">", "L", and "R" each do for values the same thing that they do for labels.

"+" results in the display of the number preceded by a "+" if positive, and by a "−" if negative. A "0", as usual, is not signed.

"−" is the usual VisiCalc mode, preceding a negative number with a "−", and leaving zero and all positive numbers alone.

"(" displays negatives in parentheses and leaves zero and all positive numbers alone.

"C" displays positive numbers with a trailing "(DR)" symbol, and a trailing "(CR)" for negative numbers. This is convenient for displaying and printing accounting reports with debits and credits.

"," displays numbers longer than four digits to the left of the decimal point with the usual non-VisiCalc "," convention. For example, 10000.23 becomes 10,000.23.

"." displays a decimal point whether or not a decimal fraction is present. The normal mode, of course, is to drop a trailing decimal point.

"Z" suppresses trailing zeros in cells with "/AVF" or "/AVS" attributes.

"%" displays a decimal fraction (or other number) as a percentage, with a trailing "%". Entry of .13 with a "/AV%" attribute will display 13%.

"$" causes a number to be preceded by a dollar sign. This attribute should not be confused with the "/F$" format command; "/AV$" does not affect the number of decimal places shown but merely displays a $.

"G" returns the "/AV" attribute to the "general" display (the usual default display). This differs from "D" (see below), which converts the display to the current global default setting.

"F" permits entry of an integer which controls how many decimals will be displayed to the right of the decimal point. This attribute includes trailing zeros (unless vetoed by the "/AVZ" attribute), and will obviously be handy for batting averages, grade point averages, stock averages and any other data where you wish to align decimal points in the same column. Before this attribute became available, it was possible to accomplish such alignment only with the "/FI" or "/F$" formats. Alignment with three trailing decimal places could not be accomplished directly.

Once again, we should stress that these attributes affect the number display only, and they do not affect the way a number is treated for further computation purposes. Use of "/AVF" will lead to "footing" problems unless the number displayed is also rounded to the same number of integers or decimal places. Conversely, it is unlikely that your numbers will line up in straight pretty columns if @ROUND is used without the "AVF" attribute.

"I" displays the indicated number in integer format, overriding "/AVZ", while "S" results in "scientific notation" of the form 1.23E3, overriding any conflicting attribute.

"*" is the same as "/F*", the so-called bar-graphing option.

Last, but not least, "D" defaults to the previously set global value attribute.

/AD DEFAULT

This final attribute option sets the indicated cell to the entire set of global default attributes last set with the "/GA" command.

CHAPTER 9

Making Life Easier

We've seen many of the new functions and formatting (attributing?) abilities of the advanced version, but VCAV also has many features which simply make VisiCalc much easier to use. Help screens; keystroke memory; variable column widths; multiple replicating; replication of attributes, values or both; and page-print formatting may not make the VCAV's output look nicer. However, they do permit the designer or user to do directly much that couldn't be done even indirectly with older versions. And they do make everyone's life a lot easier.

KEYSTROKE MEMORY

Keystroke Memory gives the designer or user the ability to assign a series of keystrokes to a single alpha key, thus designating 26 very special function keys to do just about anything. Printer-setup strings, complex attribute settings, DIF-save sequences, a simple ">A1", or virtually anything that can be described in 125 or fewer keystrokes can be executed with three keystrokes—two to enter Control-K and one for the designated letter. It really is that simple.

Keystroke memory assignments are initiated either with a "/K=" or "Control-K−", followed in each case by the single-letter "name" by which the sequence will be called in the future. The sequences that may be defined are versatile enough to delete a character, or pause and display a message on the edit line, or load an overlay file. In addition, one keystroke memory sequence can "call" another, thereby providing the ability to "chain" a sequence that is longer than 125 characters. Editing a sequence can be done using the "/KE" command. And if you forget which sequences have been defined with which

letter names, all of the defined sequences can be viewed by using the
"/K[**RETURN**]" command.

Keystroke sequences are automatically saved with a template by using the
normal "/SS" command. While it is not possible to have a set of commands
available immediately upon booting VCAV, it is possible to save a template with
defined keystroke sequences, but having no data or formulas. If such a template
is loaded with the "/SL" command at the beginning of your VCAV session, all
of your favorite keystroke sequences will thereafter be available for use.

Now that we have explained what keystroke memory is and how to use it, we
must note that it is a lot easier to use than to explain, and much more powerful
than it sounds. As with so many of the new VCAV gadgets, you will come to
depend on keystroke memory after you have gotten used to it.

Although included in the format commands rather than keystroke memory, a
special type of keystroke memory is initiated by the new "/F=" (or "/GF=")
command, which "memorizes" a series of attributes. It is easy to replicate a
complex sequence of attributes into cells that are adjacent to each other, but if
you wish a series of nonadjacent cells to show values which are left justified with
a two-space left gutter, with trailing (CR) and (DR) markings, "/F=" can be
used to set those attributes in any of the cells in question. Merely name the
"macro" with an alpha or selected nonalpha character and then type in its "definition." Placing the cursor in a cell and typing /F="name" will set that cell to
the desired format.

CLEARING MEMORY

The usual VisiCalc command to clear memory is "/CY" (Clear,Yes). "/CY"
works with VCAV, but all of the keystroke memory sequences, printer settings,
and format definitions in memory are retained. If you wish to clear all of the
memory, the proper command is "/CAY" (Clear, All, Yes). While using VCAV
for a while, you may find it helpful to retain your favorite set of special function
keys in memory and to use "/CY" rather than "/CAY" most of the time.

HELP SCREENS

Hitting the [**?**] key at just about any point in a VisiCalc operation clears the
current screen and substitutes a text "help" screen, which is designed to inform
you of the options that you have at that precise point in the program. The screen
is not the same each time you press "?", but is specifically designed for the
place in the program that you were at when you asked for help. For example,
Figure 9.1 shows the initial help screen after the sequence "/R" has been entered, while Figure 9.2 shows the help screen after "/GA" has been entered.

8: Making Life Easier

FIGURE 9.1

```
A1
Replicate (, Source Range or RETURN

A1
Information about REPLICATING A CELL OR RANGE (/R)

The Replicate command allows you to replicate a cell or range
of cells to another part of the worksheet.

( Limits what part of a cell (A for attributes only or C contents
only) is replicated or whether expression references are all
relative (R) or no change (N). RETURN or ) completes this part
of the command. Then continue by indicating the source range to
be replicated and the target range where you want the copy to
appear.

RANGE  Indicates the source range of cells to be replicated.
Both attributes and contents are replicated, unless specified
otherwise by the ( option. Type a period (.) and the coordinate
of the end of the range. RETURN completes the source range.
Indicate the target range by typing or pointing to the beginning
and ending coordinates of the range where you want the copy or
copies to appear. RETURN completes the command.

RETURN  Indicates the source to be replicated if only the cell
where the cursor lies. Both attributes and cell contents are
replicated, unless specified otherwise by the ( option. Indicate
the target range by typing or pointing

N: NEXT    ?: HELP    T: TOPICS    ESC: SHEET    C: CANCEL
```

FIGURE 9.2

```
A1 /GA
Attribute:  E H M T L V D

A1
Information about ATTRIBUTES (/A)

The Attributes command allows you to change the way cells are
displayed and control how they can be modified. Setting attri-
butes affects only the display of the cell and not the label or
value stored in memory. The VisiCalc program always retains
values at full precision and labels at the maximum buffer size.

Attribute options are:

/AE    Expression. Displays worksheet as expressions or formulas.

/AH    Hide. Hides the display, but retains any data or expressions
       in a cell.

/AL    Label. Sets label display attributes.

/AM    Mode. Specifies whether the contents of a cell can be
              modified and allows you to restrict the type of
              data that may be entered..

/AT    Tab. Specifies where the cursor will go when TAB or
            SHIFT-TAB is pressed.

/AV    Value. Sets value display attributes.

N: NEXT    ?: HELP    T: TOPICS    ESC: SHEET    C: CANCEL
```

Whenever a help screen is present, the user may enter

"N" to get the next page of help text, if any.

"P" to go back to the previous page, if any.

"T" for a list of topics which can be accessed (up and down arrows are used to select the desired topic).

[ESC] to clear the help screen and return to the VisiCalc screen, exactly where you left it.

"Control-C" to cancel both the help screen and the command or data entry that was pending at the time you pressed "?".

Oh yes, "?HELP" will display a help screen on how to use the help function. With the complications of attributes, keystroke memory, and print-page formatting added to the old VisiCalc commands, the Help screens are most welcome.

VARIABLE COLUMN WIDTHS

As every VisiCalc user learns, determining one single width as appropriate for all of the columns on a template soon becomes a matter of compromise. There is a laudable tendency to want to place long descriptive labels on the left side of the template, but such long widths are usually not required for most of the numeric areas. VCAV solves the problem and eliminates the need to compromise by permitting the designer to set any individual column to a width other than that of the globally set width.

As with earlier versions of VisiCalc, the command "/GCn", will set the width of all columns to width n, but in VCAV the new sequence "/GCCn" will now change the width only of the cursor-position column to size n characters. It is a bit inconsistent to place a nonglobal function under the "/G" command, but variable column widths are a joy to use in spite of the inconsistency.

Any number of columns may be set to a nonglobal size, and we should note that VCAV gives us the ability to change both individual or global column widths down to one character. Older versions required that columns be a minimum of three spaces wide. However, VCAV will not display numbers in a one-character-wide column size, as a number cell requires at least three spaces for a possible decimal point, a minus sign, and the number itself. Cells that will contain a "Y" or "N", or cells that will be hidden (using the "/AH" attribute) can use the one-character-wide option. Maximum column width for either individual or globally set columns is 125.

MULTIPLE REPLICATIONS AND OTHER GOODIES

VCAV permits many things to be done in big bunches. Both first- and second-stage VisiCalc, for example, permitted the designer to replicate an entire column as a source range, but they also required the designer to tell VisiCalc whether each cell reference replicated was to be replicated RELATIVE or NO CHANGE. To replicate the partial column defined starting at Cell A1 and ending at Cell A20 to the analogous cells in columns C through G, one would enter the following sequence with the cursor at Cell A1:

/R:A1...A20:C1...G1[RETURN]

At this point, the older versions of VisiCalc would ask whether each cell reference in A1 was either RELATIVE or NO CHANGE, and then replicate A1 into C1, D1, E1, F1, and G1. The program would then go to A2 and ask the same questions. VCAV gives the designer the option of typing

/R:A1...A20:C1...G1:(R

or

/R:A1...A20:C1...G1:(N

to make all of the cell references either RELATIVE or NO CHANGE.

This is nice, but unfortunately many replications have some references which are RELATIVE and others which are NO CHANGE, making this new option not quite as useful as it might first appear. It is possible, however, to define a sequence of Ns and Rs with keystroke memory and use that sequence to speed up the replication process.

In addition, VCAV includes the ability to replicate an entire block of cells contained in multiple columns and rows. Multiple copies of the replicated blocks may be made at one time in a large area of the template.

Deletions and additions of multiple rows or columns (''/IR'', or ''/DC'' for example) can be speeded up by inserting an integer before the R or C, specifying the number of rows or columns to be deleted or added. For example, ''/I10R'' will insert 10 rows at the cursor position.

We suggest that you be very careful before using this option to delete multiple rows or columns. It is very easy to unintentionally delete columns or rows containing needed information when doing the deletions one at a time. It is even easier to destroy needed data with multiple deletions. ''/DR'' will delete the cursor position row, moving everything below it up one row. Before using multiple deletes, make sure you know what you are doing, and, to be safe, save a copy of your template prior to making the deletions. A helpful feature, new with VCAV, is a request for confirmation—''Y TO DELETE''—prior to proceeding. Multiple deletions may be made even safer by specifying the range to be deleted by pointing to cell coordinates with the cursor, rather than specifying the number of rows or columns to be deleted by typing in a number. As you move the cursor to the end of the range you may view the area you are about to delete. Remember, however, that areas outside of the screen window will be deleted as well as areas within the current window. Check those areas as well before using the multiple delete.

Multiple Insertions are almost as confusing, but not quite as fatal. They won't cause a loss of data, but if you make a mistake, they may mess up your work considerably.

PAGE-PRINT FORMATTING

Both first- and second-stage VisiCalc permit printing with or without linefeeds after carriage returns and allow you to send a "printstring" of special characters to a printer. And that's it. VCAV adds numerous options to ease printing of multiple-page reports, with page numbers, titles, margin offsets, automatic page breaks, form feeds, and the like.

"/PS", or the printer setting command, permits setting of the following options:

- N: The default "/PSNL" adds a linefeed after each carriage return. "/PSNR" turns the option off. This option is the same as the "&" and "-" entries with older VisiCalcs.
- P: The default "/PSPY" prints a report with page breaks. "/PSPN" turns the option off. The usual 11-inch-long page consists of 66 lines. Allowing top and bottom margins, a report should probably not have more than 58 or 60 lines per page. The "/PSPY" option inserts page breaks if a report is longer than the number of lines specified to be printed on a page (see below), and it is inoperative if the report to be printed has fewer lines. "/PSPN" prints just as with older VisiCalcs. Note that page breaks will be inserted where VisiCalc wants to do them, not necessarily where the designer wants to do them. If your report consists of 100 lines of repetitive information; this is no problem. If, however, your report is sectioned, you certainly will not want to start a new section on the bottom line of a page. This problem is solved by turning the page option off and inserting rows as necessary, as with older VisiCalc (see Chapter 4).
- T: The default "/PSTY" prints titles on each page, if titles have previously been fixed by the "/TH", "/TV", or "/TN" commands during template design. "/PSTY" prints titles; "/PSTN" does not. Of course, if titles have not been set with the "/T" commands, no titles will be printed.
- #: The default "/PS#Y" prints page numbers. "/PS#N" turns the option off.
- L: The default "/PSL55" sets the number of lines to be printed on a page to 55. The number entered after "/PSL" must be an integer less than or equal to the specified page length.
- W: The default "/PSW70" sets the width of the line to 70 characters.
- F: The default "/PSF66" sets the page length to 66 lines. This is the usual size of an 11-inch form. Note that page length includes all of the printed

and nonprinted lines on a page. A page length of 66 and a "/PSL" default setting of 55 implies that 11 lines per page will be blank in order to provide a one-inch margin at the top and bottom of the page.

S: Insert your usual printer setup strings after "/PSS". It is necessary to do this only once for each worksheet; unlike older versions of VisiCalc, VCAV holds the printstring in memory so that it can be sent to the printer each time that you use the print command.

M: The default "/PSM0" sets the printed left margin to printer position 0. If a left-margin offset is intended, enter an integer after "/PSM".

All of the printer settings are saved when a template is saved with the "/SS" command, and they remain active until memory is cleared with the "/CAY" command. Defaults cannot be altered as such, but it is possible to create a template which consists solely of print options, keystroke memories, and format strings, or any combination thereof, and then to load that template when starting to work.

TO BUY OR NOT TO BUY?

Such is the advanced version of VisiCalc. There is no question in our minds that if you are even a moderate user of VisiCalc, VCAV is worth the price differential and even the upgrade price—at this writing, $150 and $200, respectively. We have not yet decided whether it is worth the price of an upgraded computer just to use VCAV. But we do hope that VCAV will become available for all of the computers currently using second-stage VisiCalc, without requiring substantial equipment modifications or enhancements.

APPENDIXES

A. Command Reference Guide
B. Function Reference Guide
C. The Blank Model Template
D. DocuCalc Template Printout

APPENDIX A

Command Reference Guide

This section of *Dynamics of VisiCalc* is intended to supplement the VisiCalc manual by supplying a concise explanation of what each command does, how to use it, and what to watch out for. Other sections of *Dynamics of VisiCalc* discuss these matters in greater detail. The Appendix does not include the advanced version of VisiCalc.

VisiCalc's operating commands are discussed in the context of your computer's operation in its VisiCalc manual. The VisiCalc command structure chart, printed in the VisiCalc manual, as well as the manual itself, should be consulted to solve problems concerned with your particular computer.

The phrase "cursor cell" as used in this command reference section, means the cell that is currently being "pointed to" by the cursor. The cursor cell may be highlighted in reverse video, or with brackets, depending on the capabilities of your computer. The phrase "cursor position" refers to the column and row identified by the coordinates of the cursor cell. Thus, if the cursor cell is G5, the number of the cursor position row is 5, and the cursor position column is G.

/B BLANK

Erases, or "blanks," the current value or label from the cursor cell. "/B" will not change local formatting, which can only be returned to the current global default format with the "/FD" command.

/CY   CLEAR SCREEN

Clears the current VisiCalc workspace of all labels, values, numbers, and local formats. It also changes the global commands to their respective defaults. Use "/CY" when starting to design a new template or when loading a new template into memory.

When "/C" is entered, VisiCalc requests confirmation to be sure that you do not erase the template in memory by accident. "Y" (for "yes") will complete the command. Any other key will cancel the command.

/D   DELETE

Requires an additional keystroke entry, "R" to delete a row or "C" to delete a column.

/DR   DELETE ROW

Deletes the row of the cursor position, thereby deleting all formulas, numbers, labels, and local formats that were contained in the row. All rows below the deleted row are moved up one row position. Cell references and functions taking ranges as arguments (for example, @SUM, @AVERAGE, and @NPV) are adjusted to relocate the appropriate cell reference or to narrow the range, unless the deleted row is specifically referenced or named as the beginning or ending of the range. If the deleted row is specifically mentioned in a formula, the cell reference will be replaced by @ERROR, and the correct reference must be entered before the template will function properly.

/DC   DELETE COLUMN

Deletes the column of the cursor position, clearing all information that may have been contained in the column. All columns to the right of the deleted column are moved one column position to the left. Cell references and functions taking ranges as arguments (for example, @SUM, @AVERAGE, and @NPV) are adjusted to relocate the appropriate cell reference or to narrow the range, unless the deleted column is specifically referenced or named as the beginning or ending of the range. If the deleted column is specifically mentioned in a formula, the cell reference will be replaced by @ERROR, and the correct reference must be entered before the template will function properly.

/E   EDIT

Places the contents of the cursor cell on the edit line, so that the user can modify the line. In general, left and right arrows will move the edit cursor to the left and right, and the escape key will delete the character immediately to the left of the edit cursor. The exact method of editing is machine dependent. Consult your VisiCalc manual for specifics.

At the successful conclusion of "/E", the edited cell is recalculated, even if VisiCalc is in the manual recalculation mode (see "/GR"). The sequence "/E [RETURN]" can be used to determine the current value of a cell without recalculating the entire template. Note, however, that the recalculation may not be accurate, because, the recalculation may be using noncurrent information in cells referenced by the edited cell.

/F FORMAT

Changes the format in the cursor cell only. /F affects only the way the cursor cell is displayed and does not affect the actual value or label in the cell. Because the format commands do not change the actual numeric value in a cell, and all values are carried in exact decimal fraction form, it is possible to have results of a calculation appear to be incorrect if only the displays of the manipulated cells are observed. If you want to display a number in either integers or dollars and cents, and "the appearance of accuracy" is important, the cell in question should be rounded.

Only one format is permitted in a cell. Thus, it is not possible to have a left-justified number in integer format. Local formats always override global formats. The last-entered format will override previously entered formats.

/FD FORMAT DEFAULT

Sets the cell format to the current global format (see "/GF"). A "/FD" must be entered after a "/B" to completely eliminate a previously utilized cell which contained a local format.

/FG FORMAT GENERAL

The default formats established when VisiCalc is booted. Labels are left justified and are displayed to the extent of the column width. Values, including Booleans, are right justified with a leading blank on the left, and to the maximum possible number of significant digits to the right of the decimal point. Numeric values are automatically switched to scientific notation as necessary to best display the value.

/FI FORMAT INTEGER

Display a numeric value to the nearest whole number. It does not affect the actual value retained in the cell for future computation.

/FL FORMAT LEFT JUSTIFIED

Affects only values, as labels are already left justified in the general format. If the number in a cell is too large for, or exactly matches, the column width, "/FL" will have no noticeable effect.

/FR FORMAT RIGHT JUSTIFIED

Affects only labels, as values are already right justified in the general format. A label which is the same size as, or larger than, the current column width will not be visibly affected.

/F$ FORMAT DOLLARS AND CENTS

Rounds the display of numeric values to exactly two trailing decimal places. Nonsignificant zeroes to the right of the decimal place are always displayed. Note that the actual value retained in the cell for future computation is not changed.

/F* FORMAT BAR GRAPH

Returns the number of asterisks ("*") equal to the integer portion of the value in the cell, to a maximum of one "*" fewer than the current column width. (Both 1.1 and 1.9 are represented as "*", 6.8 is represented by "******", and .999 is represented by a seemingly blank cell.)

/G GLOBAL

Commands commenced by "/G" affect all cells on the VisiCalc template. However, a local format in a cell will take precedence over a global format. The entry of "/FD" (default format) within the cell will return the local cell to the global format command. The global command defaults listed below refer to the setting of the command when VisiCalc is first run, or after a "/CY" command is executed.

/GC COLUMN WIDTH

Changes the width of all columns to the number of characters entered immediately after the command (3 to 37 on the standard Apple II, 3 to 77 on an 80-column IBM Personal Computer). Variable column widths are not implemented on the standard version of VisiCalc. "/GC" affects, not only the column width shown on the screen, but also the column width printed to disk or to printer (using "/PP", "/PD", or "/PF" commands). Column width default is 9.

/GO ORDER OF RECALCULATION

Determines the order in which a VisiCalc template is recalculated. The order of calculation is shown in the upper right-hand corner of the screen, an R for row order, and a C for column order. Recalculation always begins with Cell A1 and proceeds either across Row 1 to BK1 before beginning with A2 (row order of calculation initiated by the command "/GOR") or proceeds down all of Column A to A254 before beginning with Cell B1 (column order of calculation initiated by the command "/GOC"). An improper choice of order of recalculation can result in forward or circular references and can lead to faulty output. Recalculation defaults to column order.

/GF GLOBAL FORMAT

Changes the format of all cells which have local default formats (no local format, or "/FD"). "/GF" requires a third entry, identical to the choices under local formats: D, G, I, L, R, or $. See discussion of the "/F" command. "/GFG" and "/GFD" appear identical.

/I INSERT

Requires an additional argument "R", for insertion of a blank row, or "C", for insertion of a blank column.

/IR INSERT ROW

Inserts a blank row at the cursor position and moves all data in the previous cursor position down one row. Data above the cursor position remain unchanged. Cell references and functions taking ranges as arguments (for example, @SUM, @AVERAGE, and @NPV) are adjusted to account for the relocated cell reference or to expand the range.

/IC INSERT COLUMN

Inserts a blank column at the cursor position and moves all data in the column previously at or to the right of the cursor one column to the right. Data to the left of the cursor stay in place. Cell references and functions taking ranges as arguments (for example, @SUM, @AVERAGE, and @NPV) are adjusted to account for the relocated cell reference or to expand the range.

/M   MOVE

Moves an entire column or row from the cursor position to the row or column specified in answer to VisiCalc's "To:" prompt. The specified cell must be in the same row or column as the cursor position. If in the same row, the cursor position column will be moved; if in the same column, the cursor position row will be moved. Moving down or to the right is confusing.

For example, if the cursor position is C3, and the cell reference C17, Rows 4 through 16 will become Rows 3 through 15 and Row 3 will be moved to Row 16. If the Cell reference is M3, Column C will be moved to Column L, and Columns D through L will become Columns C through K. A response which is not in either the same row or column as the cursor position will not be accepted.

/P   PRINT

Outputs the contents of the cells in a specified rectangular area of the template, in the format and column widths displayed on the screen. It does not print formulas, labels to the extent that they are longer than the established column width, or the actual values of numbers as calculated, unaffected by format commands. Each outputted line is terminated by a carriage return, but there is no separation between adjacent cells other than such spaces as may be present in the cells themselves. "/P" requires the user to specify an output destination which may be either a disk file or printer. The cursor must be on the upper left-hand corner of the rectangle to be printed when the command is initiated, and the lower right-hand cell of the rectangle to be printed must be specified after any required "setup strings" are issued.

/PP   PRINT TO PRINTER

Outputs a rectangular area of the template to printer. This is the standard command for printing all or a portion of the VisiCalc template for report purposes. If VisiCalc does not recognize your printer interface, it may be necessary to specify the interface's location. On the Apple II, for example, it is necessary with some interface cards to specify a slot number rather than simply "P" or **[RETURN]** for "printer." In such cases, the command is "/P1", if the printer interface card is located in slot number 1.

After "/PP" or "/P1", VisiCalc will prompt for "Setup String", "-", "&", or "lower right". If your printer requires control characters or other instructions to print your report, enter a quotation mark followed by your string. Enter a carot (∧) followed by the appropriate letter as follows:

Character Type	Enter
Control	C (Character)
Escape	E
Hexadecimal number	H (number)
Linefeed	L
Carriage return	R

Thus a standard instruction to widen the printing area of a Centronics printer to 80 characters would be entered:

∧CI80N (Control−I80N)

Consult your printer manual and interface manual to determine if a setup string is required. Some interface cards and printers will "store" the setup string, requiring it to be entered only once per printing session. You must test your particular equipment to determine whether the string must be entered each time you print, or whether it is saved from time to time as long as VisiCalc is in operation. More than one setup string may be entered if required, but each string must be initiated with a quotation mark and terminated by a carriage return.

When all setup strings have been entered, the user can instruct VisiCalc to delete its usual carriage return ("-") or add an extra carriage return ("&"). These commands are remembered by VisiCalc and need be entered only once per session. The lower right of the rectangle must be specified, usually by "pointing" to it with the cursor, and printing may begin.

/PF OR /PD   PRINT TO DISK

Outputs a rectangular area of the template to a disk file. VisiCalc requests a filename and the lower right corner of the area to be "printed." Once saved, the "printed" file may be used by other programs, such as word processors, or it may be communicated to other computers via telephone lines, but it may not be used again by VisiCalc, except in the special VisEXEC usage (see Chapter 4).

/R   REPLICATE

Reproduces the label, number, or formula in one cell or a range of cells (the source range), so that it is repeated in another cell or range of cells (the target range). Thus, the formula in Cell C20 can be transferred to D20, E20, F20, G20, and H20 with just a few keystrokes.

"/R" prompts for the source range, a single cell, or a group of adjacent cells in the same row or column. The source range usually begins at the cursor position. VisiCalc then prompts for the beginning and end of the target range, which again may be a single cell or may include a group of adjacent cells in the same row or column.

If the source range is a single cell, the target range may be a single cell or a portion of a row or column.

If the source range is a portion of a column, the target range should be either a single cell—if you wish to replicate to one column only—or a section of a row—if you wish to replicate to a series of adjacent columns. Replication will not work properly if you specify both the target and source ranges to be portions of a column.

If the source range is a portion of a row, the target range should be either a single cell—if you wish to replicate to one row only—or a section of a column—if you wish to replicate to a series of adjacent rows. Replication will not work properly if you specify both the target and source ranges to be portions of a row.

Numbers and labels are copied from the source range to the target range automatically. But if the source range contains a formula with cell references, VisiCalc highlights each reference, one at a time, and requires the user to specify whether the target range should contain the same cell reference with "no change" ("N"), or should have the same position relative to the target cell as to the Source Cell—that is, "relative" ("R"). Thus, if Cell C20 contains a reference to Cell C1, and the replication to D20...G20 is marked as "R", D20 will contain D1, E20, E1, and so forth. If the replication is specified as "N", however, D20...G20 will each contain the reference to C1.

/S STORAGE

Initiates an extensive submenu for disk (and in some instances cassette tape) input and output of VisiCalc templates, and also enables limited file housekeeping.

/SQ QUIT

Permits the user to gracefully exit from VisiCalc and cause the system to reboot. A disk with the computer's standard disk operating system should be placed in the boot drive prior to initiating this command.

/SS SAVE

Saves the entire template to the output device. The process begins in the lower right corner, proceeds across each row to the leftmost cell in the row, and then continues at the rightmost cell of the next-higher row. One can save uncalculated formulas, unformatted numbers, and complete labels as well as information regarding the location of the cell and local format. A typical cell may be saved as follows:

$$>B5:/F\$(A1+1)$$

This informs VisiCalc that the formula "A1+1", with a dollars-and-cents local format, is saved in Cell B5.

The entry use of quotation marks,

$$>B5:/F\$"(A1+1)$$

would show the entry in question to be a label. After saving information as to each cell, VisiCalc saves information as to column width, order of recalculation, automatic or manual recalculation, windowing, titling, and the location of the screen and cursor.

/SS FILENAME   SAVE TO DISK

Saves the entire template to a disk file with the name FILENAME. FILENAME may later be loaded into VisiCalc with a "/SL FILENAME" command.

/SS,S(SLOTNUMBER)   SAVE TO PRINTER
(Apple II only)

Saves (prints) the entire template to printer, in a line-by-line format, exactly the way a template is saved to disk. The resulting printout can be used to view template logic as a whole. (See the manual for your machine.)

/SL   LOAD FILE FROM DISK

Loads a template previously saved by a "/SS FILENAME" command. If VisiCalc's work area has not previously been cleared, "/SL" will alter only the cells containing data in the loaded template. Cells not containing data in the loaded template will continue to hold previously existing information.

/SI   INITIALIZE DISK

Formats disk. However, it is machine dependent and may not be present on all versions. The Apple II version formats an unbootable disk, which can save data on tracks 1 to 34 but not on track 0. DOS is not placed on the disk, and therefore two additional tracks (1 and 2) are available for data storage. This command will destroy all information previously recorded on the disk.

/S#   DIF STORAGE

Initiates saves and loads of rectangular portions of a template in data interchange format.

/S#S   DIF-SAVE

The cursor should be moved to the upper left-hand corner of the rectangular area to be saved. VisiCalc first requests a filename and a format ("C", "R", or "Return") and then prompts for the coordinates of the lower right corner of the rectangular area to be saved. "C" saves the data from the top to the bottom of the first column, and then to the top of the next, and so forth. "R" and "Return" are identical and save information from left to right in the first row.

The DIF operation saves data only. Formulas and cell references are replaced by their calculated numeric values. Global commands and local cell formats are not saved.

/S#L   DIF-LOAD

The cursor should be moved to upper left-hand corner of the rectangular area to which the data will be loaded. This need not be the same area from which the data was originally saved. VisiCalc will request a filename and the loading format. "C" loads data in column format. "R" or "Return" loads data in row format. If the load format is the same as the format that was used when the file was saved, the loaded data will be arranged the same way as the original data that were DIF-saved. If the save format was "C", and the load format "R" or "Return" (or the save format "R" or "Return" and the load format "C"), the data will be rotated 90 degrees. Numeric values and labels will be returned to the template.

Figure A.1 represents data from a portion of a template. Figure A.2 represents the same data, DIF-saved with "C" format, and DIF-loaded in "R" format. The result would be the same if Figure A.1 had been DIF-saved with "R" format and DIF-loaded with "C" format.

FIGURE A.1

```
              COLUMN 1  COLUMN 2
    ROW 1       110       120
    ROW 2       210       220
    ROW 3       310       320
    ROW 4       410       420
    ROW 5       510       520
    ROW 6       610       620
```

FIGURE A.2

	ROW 1	ROW 2	ROW 3	ROW 4	ROW 5	ROW 6
COLUMN 1	110	210	310	410	510	610
COLUMN 2	120	220	320	420	520	620

/T TITLES

Creates a barrier through which the cursor cannot be scrolled and freezes cells on the screen even though the cursor is scrolled beyond the normal range of the barrier. Titles may be used to ease entry and comprehension of data on the limited size of the VisiCalc screen. There is no visible delineation between the "locked" title areas and the scrollable data. Titles may be lost after execution of a ">" command far off screen, above or to the left of the cursor position.

Titles may also be used in connection with the "Windows" command ("/W") to obtain four or more separate areas on your VisiCalc screen at one time.

/TH HORIZONTAL TITLES

Creates a barrier at the current row of the cursor position. All rows at or above the current cursor position row will remain on the VisiCalc screen. For example, the command sequence

>Z50
/TH
>Z51

will establish a horizontal barrier at Row 50, preventing the cursor from scrolling above Row 51. Scrolling down, or "going to" D100, will result in all cells at Row 50 and above remaining in the same position as prior to the scroll or ">". However the command sequence

>A1
>AA51

may destroy the established horizontal titles.

/TV VERTICAL TITLES

Creates a barrier at the cursor position column. All columns at or to the left of the cursor position column will remain on the VisiCalc screen.

For example, the command sequence

>Z50
/TV
>AA51

will establish a vertical barrier at Column Z, preventing the cursor from scrolling to the left of column AA. Scrolling down, or "going to" AX100, will result in all cells at Column Z and to the left remaining in the same position as prior to the scroll or ">". However the command sequence

>A1
>AA51

may destroy the established vertical titles.

/TB   (BOTH) VERTICAL AND HORIZONTAL TITLES

Combines "/TH" and "/TV" (see below). It sets a vertical barrier at the cursor position column and a horizontal barrier at the cursor position row.

/V   VERSION

Displays the version identification and disk serial number on the entry line.

/W   WINDOW

Controls division of the VisiCalc screen into two "windows". Hitting the [;] key will switch cursor from one window to the other. Column width and direction of cursor movement (on the Apple II) can be different for each screen, but recalculations on one screen will affect the other window, also.

/WH   HORIZONTAL WINDOW

Divides the VisiCalc screen horizontally into two windows with the division at the cursor position row. The division is indicated by a visible bar containing the column identification letters for each column in the second window.

/WV   VERTICAL WINDOW

Divides the VisiCalc screen vertically into two windows, with the division more or less at the right of the cursor position column. The division is indicated by a visible bar containing the row identification numbers for each row in the second window.

/WS SYNCHRONIZED WINDOW SCROLLING

Coordinates scrolling between the two window screens if present. With a vertical window, the two screens will move up and down together. With a horizontal window, the two screens will move right and left together.

/WU UNSYNCHRONIZED WINDOW SCROLLING

Prevents movement of one window (vertically or horizontally) when the other window is being moved. The user can "freeze" one portion of the template display and view another portion at the same time. "/WU" is the default.

/W1 RESTORE SINGLE DISPLAY

Reverses a "/WH" or "/WV" instruction. Column size, cursor direction, and cursor position will continue from the screen containing the cursor at the time the command is issued.

REPEATING LABEL

Takes the character or string of characters following the command and prior to a [RETURN], and repeats the sequence across the entire cell. This technique is often used for "dressing up" formatted displays and printouts. The label may be a single character such as *, -, =, :, A, or Z, or a series of characters such as *-=:AZ. The single character or series will be repeated to the extent of the column width.

> GOTO

Positions the cursor on the cell specified after the command. The cursor moves directly to the specified cell, and the VisiCalc screen is rewritten without scrolling.

APPENDIX B

Function Reference Guide

This Appendix contains each of the built-in functions present in second-stage VisiCalc along with syntax for use of the function and a practical illustration of how it may be used. Many of the functions include a typical problem and solutions to the problem using that function. The first solution is a high-level English-like metalanguage format we have called Hi-Calc, and the second solution is in VisiCalc template format. You should be able to read and understand the "Hi-Calc solution" without problem and to use the Hi-Calc as a bridge to understanding of the VisiCalc solution.

Beneath many of the VisiCalc template illustrations, we have sketched the VisiCalc keystrokes necessary to duplicate the portion of the template concerned with the function under discussion. Where replications are required, we have indicated the source and target ranges, where necessary, and whether the replicated cell references are no change ("N") or relative ("R"). Some examples use formatting which is not indicating.

@ABS

Syntax: @ABS*(variable)*

Translation: Returns the value of *variable* without regard to *variable*'s sign, that is, the absolute value of *variable*.

Problem: Determine, for purposes of an exception report, whether sales vary from budget by more than 10 percent. Answer TRUE if the variance is greater than 10 percent; Answer FALSE if the variance is 10 percent or less.

Hi-Calc: (@ABS((SALES − BUDGET)/BUDGET)>.1

VisiCalc:

	B	C	D
2		ANDY	BETTY
3	SALES	15687	18687
4	QUOTA	15000	15000
5			
6	OK?	FALSE	TRUE

>C6:(@ABS((C3-C4)/C4)>.1
>D6:(@ABS((D3-D4)/D4)>.1

@ACOS

Syntax: @ACOS(*variable*)

Translation: Returns the size, expressed in radians, of an angle with cosine of size *variable*.

Problem: Calculate the size, in both radians and degrees, of an angle with a given cosine.

Hi-Calc: @ACOS(0)=1.5707963268 radians
@ACOS(0)*(360/(2*@PI)=90 degrees

VisiCalc:

	B	C	D
2		COSINE	ARCOSINE	ARCOSINE
3	57.29578	(RADIANS)	(DEGREES)
4	==========================
5	-1.1	ERROR	ERROR
6	-1	3.141593	180.00
7	-.5	2.094395	120.00
8	0	1.570796	90.00
9	.5	1.047198	60.00
10	1	0	0.00
11	1.1	ERROR	ERROR

>B3:(360/(2*@PI))
>C5:@ACOS(B5)
>C5:/R:C6.C11:R
>D5:(@ACOS(B5)*B3)
>D5:/R:D6.D11:RN

Note: B3 represents the conversion factor from radians to degrees, being the number of degrees per radian.

B: Function Reference Guide

User Note: All direct answers will be in radians. *Variable* must be in the range -1 to $+1$, or @ACOS will return ERROR.

@AND

Syntax: @AND(*condition1, condition2,...conditionN*)

Translation: Returns TRUE if each *condition* is TRUE, and returns FALSE if any *condition* is not TRUE.

Problem: A salesperson becomes eligible for a bonus by producing total sales 10 percent or more over budget, and as long as sales for neither of the two products being purveyed are under budget. Answer TRUE if the commission has been earned. Answer FALSE if it has not.

Hi-Calc: @AND ((Sales.Total / Budget.Total)> 1.1, Sales.Product1 > = Budget.Product1, Sales.Product2 > = Budget.Product2)

VisiCalc:

	A	B	C	D	E	F	G
2			ANDY		BETTY		CHARLES
3		SALES	BUDGET	SALES	BUDGET	SALES	BUDGET
4	PROD 1	1010	1000	800	800	1099	1100
5	PROD 2	1450	1400	1350	1120	2000	1540
6		------	------	------	------	------	------
7	TOTAL	2460	2400	2150	1920	3099	2640
8							
9		BONUS?	FALSE	BONUS?	TRUE	BONUS?	FALSE

>C9:@AND(B7/C7>=1.1, B4>=C4,B5>=C5)
>C9:/R:E9:RRRRRR
>C9:/R:G9:RRRRRR

User Note: @AND will accept multiple Boolean conditions as arguments. If a condition has the value NA, @AND will return NA. Any other value (including blank, a number, or ERROR) will return ERROR.

@ASIN

Syntax: @ASIN(*variable*)

Translation: Returns the size, expressed in radians, of an angle with sine *variable*.

Problem: Calculate the size, in radians and degrees, of an angle with a given sine.

Hi-Calc: @ASIN(−1,)=−1.57080 radians
@ASIN(−1)*(360/(2*@PI)=−90.00 degrees

VisiCalc:

	B	C	D
2	SINE	ARCSINE	ARCSINE
3	57.29578	(RADIANS)	(DEGREES)
4	==============================		
5	-1.1	ERROR	ERROR
6	-1	-1.57080	-90.00
7	-.5	-.523599	-30.00
8	0	0	0.00
9	.5	.5235988	30.00
10	1	1.570796	90.00
11	1.1	ERROR	ERROR

>B3:(360/(2*@PI)
>C5:@ASIN(B5)
>C5:/R:C6.C11:R
>D5:(@ASIN(B5))*B3
>D5:/R:D6.D11:RN

User Note: All direct answers will be in radians. *Variable* must be in the range −1 to +1, or @ASIN will return the value ERROR.

@ATAN

Syntax: @ATAN(*variable*)

Translation: Returns the size, expressed in radians, of the angle with tangent *variable*.

Problem: Calculate the size, in radians and degrees, of angle with a given tangent.

Hi-Calc: @ATAN(−200)=−1.5657964 radians
@ATAN(-200)*(360/(2*@PI)=−89.71 degrees

VisiCalc:

	B	C	D
2	ARCTANGENT	ARCTANGENT	ARCTANGENT
3	57.2957795	(RADIANS)	(DEGREES)
4	==============================		
5	-200	-1.5657964	-89.71
6	-100	-1.5607967	-89.43
7	-10	-1.4711277	-84.29
8	0	0	0.00
9	10	1.47112767	84.29
10	100	1.56079666	89.43
11	200	1.56579637	89.71

B: Function Reference Guide

>B3:(360/(2*@PI)
>C5:@ATAN(B5)
>D5:@ATAN(B5)*(B3)
>C5:/R:C6.C11:R
>D5:/R:D6.D11:RN

@AVERAGE

Syntax: @AVERAGE*(beginrange...endrange)*
@AVERAGE*(element1,element2...elementN)*

Translation: Calculate the mean average of the values contained in a given range or internal list of cells.

Problem: Calculate the average daily sales for a week, for each salesperson, and the average sales for each day, for all the salespersons.

Hi-Calc: @AVERAGE(Sales-Monday ... Sales-Friday)

VisiCalc:

	B	C	D	E	F	G	H
3	SALESMAN:	MONDAY	TUESDAY	WEDNESDAY	THURSDAY	FRIDAY	AVERAGE
4	ANDY	1021	579	1200	1423	1232	1091.00
5	BETTY	1200	322		1700	500	930.50
6	CHARLES	321	500	1234	340	456	570.20
7	DAVID	1421	321	994	423	1204	872.60
8	EDWARD	1211	121	321	123	2030	761.20
9	FRANK	1009	900	1400	100	1240	929.80
10							
11	AVERAGE:	1030.50	457.17	1029.80	684.83	1110.33	859.22
12							
13							
14							

>C11:@AVERAGE(C4.C9)
>C11:/R:D11.H11:RR
>H4:@AVERAGE(C4.G4)
>H4:/R:H5.H9:RR

User Note: A blank cell or a cell with a label within a list or range will not be counted as part of the denominator. If a cell within the range or list is NA, @AVERAGE will return NA. If a cell within a range or list has a Boolean value, @AVERAGE will return ERROR. @AVERAGE is the equivalent of @SUM/@COUNT. An individual cell within a list will be counted as part of the denominator even though it may be blank.

@CHOOSE

SYNTAX: @CHOOSE(*argument, element1, element2...elementN*)
@CHOOSE(*argument, beginrange...endrange*)

Translation: Return the element of the list or range which is equal to the position in the list or range specified by *argument*. Any decimal fractions of *argument* are truncated.

Problem: Items 1, 2, 3, 4, and 5 are for sale at prices of $1.50, $2.65, $3.95, $2.00, and $1.59, respectively. Determine, for purposes of invoice extension, the price for each item as entered in the invoice.

Hi-Calc: @CHOOSE(Item-Number,$1.50, $2.65, $3.95, $2.00, $1.59)

VisiCalc:

	B	C	D	E
2		INVOICE		
3	======	==========	=======	========
4	ITEM	QUANTITY	PRICE	TOTAL
5	2	23	2.65	60.95
6	3	17	3.95	67.15
7	1	11	1.50	16.50
8	4	1	2.00	2.00
9	5	13	1.59	20.67
10				------
11				167.27

>D5:@CHOOSE(B5,1.5,2.65,3.95,2,1.59)
>D5:/R:D6.D9:R

As an alternative

>A20:1.5
>A21:2.65
>A22:3.95
>A23:2
>A24:1.59
>D5:@CHOOSE(B5,A20...A24)
>D5:/R:D6...D9:RNN

User Note: @CHOOSE will return values only, and not labels. If *argument* is not an integer, the *chosen* number will be equal to @INT(*argument*). @CHOOSE and @LOOKUP are similar in operation, except that @LOOKUP cannot use an internal list but will only operate within a specified range, and @CHOOSE requires that *argument* be a number no larger than the number of elements in the list or range.

@COS

Syntax: @COS(*variable*)

Translation: Returns the cosine of angle of size *variable*.

Problem: Calculate the cosine of an angle with given size. Angle may be expressed in degrees or radians.

Hi-Calc: @COS(−10 radians)=0.84
@COS(−90 degrees)*(2@PI)

VisiCalc:

	B	C	D	E	F	G
2		57.29578			.0174533	
3	ANGLE	ANGLE	COSINE	ANGLE	ANGLE	COSINE
4	(RADIANS)	(DEGREES)		(DEGREES)	(RADIANS)	
5	−10	−572.958	−.839072	−90	−1.57080	0
6	−5	−286.479	.2836622	−45	−.785398	.7071068
7	−1	−57.2958	.5403023	−30	−.523599	.8660254
8	−.5	−28.6479	.8775826	−15	−.261799	.9659258
9	−.25	−14.3239	.9689124	0	0	1
10	0	0	1	30	.5235988	.8660254
11	.25	14.32394	.9689124	60	1.047198	.5000000
12	.5	28.64789	.8775826	75	1.308997	.2588190
13	1	57.29578	.5403023	90	1.570796	0
14	10	572.9578	−.839072	180	3.141593	−1
15						

>C2:(180/@PI)
>F2:@PI/180
>C5:(B5*C2)
>D5:@COS(B5)
>F5:(E5*F2)
>G5:@COS(F5)
>C5:/R:C6.C14:RN
>D5:/R:D6.D14:R
>F5:/R:F6.F14:RN
>G5:/R:G6.G14:R

User Note: Angle size *variable* must be expressed in radians.

@COUNT

Syntax: @COUNT(*beginrange...endrange*) or
@COUNT(*element1, element2...elementN*)

Translation: Calculate the number of nonblank elements in the list or range.

Problem: Determine the number of salespersons who made *any* sales on a given day.

Hi-Calc: @COUNT (Firstsalesperson...Lastsalesperson)

VisiCalc:

	B	C	D	E
2	SALESMAN	MONDAY	TUESDAY	WEDNESDAY
3	ANDY	3		1
4	BETTY		3	1
5	CHARLES	1		
6	DAVID	4	1	
7	EDWARD	2		2
8		=======	=======	=======
9		4	2	3

>C9:@COUNT(C3.C7)
>C9:/R:D9.E9:RR

User Note: Referencing an empty list will result in 0, but not an error condition. A blank cell or a cell with a label will not be "counted," but a cell with a Boolean value, including NA or ERROR, will be "counted."

@ERROR

Syntax: @ERROR

Translation: Returns the value ERROR.

User Note: Use @ERROR to notify the user of an error condition in the template input which is not considered erroneous by VisiCalc itself. For example, @ERROR can notify the user that a given input is outside of a required range of values.

@EXP

Syntax: @EXP*(variable)*

Translation: Returns ($e \wedge variable$).

Problem: Calculate the value of *e* to a given power.

Solution: @EXP(142) = 4.6753747837E61

User Note: *Variable* greater than 142.76 or less that −151.95, or a nonnumeric value, will return ERROR.

@FALSE

Syntax: @FALSE

Translation: Returns the value FALSE.

@IF

Syntax: @IF*(condition, expression1, expression2)*

Translation: IF *condition* is TRUE, evaluate *expression1*, ELSE, if *condition* is FALSE, evaluate *expression2*.

Problem: Calculate the commission for each salesperson at 10 percent of sales if sales are over $6,000, at 6 percent of sales if sales are $6,000 or less, but more than $4,000, at 4 percent if sales are over $1,000 but $4,000 or less, and no commission if sales are $1,000 or less.

Hi-Calc: @IF (Sales < 1000 THEN no commission;
ELSE, @IF sales <=4000 then 4 percent*sales;
ELSE, @IF sales <=6000 then 6 percent*sales;
ELSE, @IF sales then 10 percent*sales.

VisiCalc:

	B	C	D
2	SALESMAN	SALES	COMMISSION
3	================================		
4	ANDY	2350	94
5	BETTY	12500	1250
6	CHARLES	NA	NA
7	DAVID	4700	282
8	EDWARD	700	0
9	FRANK	1300	52

>D4:@IF(C4<1000,0,@IF(C4<4000,.04*C4,@IF(C4<6000,C4*.06,C4*.1)
>D4:/R:D5.D9:RRRRRR

User Note: Conditions must evaluate as TRUE or FALSE, and may be Boolean *variables* or references to cells with Booleans. @IFs may be nested, as shown in above.

@INT

Syntax: @INT*(variable)*

Translation: Returns the "whole number" portion of *variable,* dropping all numbers to the right of the decimal point.

Problem: Round the positive number in cells in column A to three decimal places, to the nearest integer, and to the nearest 50.

Hi-Calc: 3 places: *Rounded number* = **INT(*number**1000+.5)/1000**

Integer: *Rounded number* = **INT(*number*+.5)**

50s: *Rounded number* = **INT((*number*/50)+25)*50**

VisiCalc:

	A	B	C	D
1	NUMBERS	3 PLACES	INTEGERS	THOUSANDS
2	========	========	========	========
3	12344.32123	12344.321	12344	12000
4	12562.09999	12562.1	12562	13000
5	10903	10903	10903	11000
6	999.01321	999.013	999	1000
7	750.1111	750.111	750	1000
8	499.9999	500	500	0
9	1	1	1	0

>B3:@INT(A3*1000+.5)/1000
>C3:@INT(A3+.5)
>D3:@INT(A3/1000+.5)*1000
>B3:/R:B4.B9:R
>C3:/R:C4.C9:R
>D3:/R:D4.D9:R

@ISERROR

Syntax: @ISERROR*(cell reference)*

Translation: Returns TRUE if cell reference evaluates as ERROR, and returns FALSE if cell reference does not evaluate as ERROR.

B: Function Reference Guide

Problem: Test to determine whether a "divide by zero" error will result, and set answer to 0 instead of permitting ERROR value.

Hi-Calc: IF @ISERROR (Sales.Dollars/Sales.Units) is TRUE, display 0.

VisiCalc:

	B	C	D	E
2	SALESMAN	SALES	SALES	AVERAGE
3		(DOLLARS)	(UNITS)	($/UNITS)
4	===
5	ANDY	944	11	85.82
6	BETTY	576	7	82.29
7	CHARLES	1100	14	78.57
8	DAVID	0	0	0.00
9	EDWARD	754	3	251.33
10				
11				

>E5:@IF(@ISERROR(C5/D5,0,C5/D5)
>E5:/R:E6.E9:RRRR

User Note: Any value, label, Boolean, (including NA) except the value of ERROR results in FALSE.

@ISNA

Syntax: @ISNA*(cell reference)*

Translation: Returns TRUE if *cell reference* is NA, and returns FALSE if *cell reference* is not NA.

User Note: Any value, label, Boolean (including ERROR) results in FALSE.

@LN

Syntax: @LN*(variable)*

Translation: Returns the natural logarithm (to base "e") of *variable*.

Example: @LN(50) RETURNS: 3.9120230053

User Note: *Variable* must be greater than zero. A zero or negative value of *variable* will return ERROR.

@LOG10

Syntax: @LOG10(*variable*)

Translation: Returns the logarithm (to base 10) of *variable*.

Example : @LOG10(50) RETURNS:1.6989700043

User Note: *Variable* must be greater than zero. A zero or negative value of *variable* will return ERROR.

@LOOKUP

Syntax: @LOOKUP(*variable, beginrange...endrange*)
@LOOKUP(*cell reference, beginrange...endrange*)

Translation: Identify the cell in *beginrange...endrange* (the *range*) with a value equal to *variable* (or the value of *cell reference*.) If *variable* does not match any entry in *range* then identify the cell in *range* that has the largest value in *range* that is less than *variable*. Return the value of the cell immediately to the right of the identified cell if *range* is in a column, or immediately below the identified cell if the *range* is in a row.

Problem: Calculate the federal income tax, according to the tax rate schedule if over $50,000 and according to the tax charts if less than $50,000, payable by a married couple filing a joint return for the calendar year 1982.

Hi-Calc: @LOOKUP(*income,starttable...endtable*)

VisiCalc:

	A	B	C	D	E
92	TAXABLE INCOME:>>>>>>>>$		20932.32	TAX:$	3118.25
93			BASE LEVEL		
94		INCOME	TAX		
95					
96	20925.00	0.00	0.00		
97		3400.00	2103		
98		5500.00	2412		
99		7600.00	2678		
100		11900.00	2949		
101		16000.00	3097		
102		20200.00	3118		
103		24600.00	2971		
104		29900.00	2612		
105		35200.00	1756		
106		45800.00	512		
107		60000.00	-1442		
108		85600.00	-2089		
109		1E12	ERROR		

B: Function Reference Guide

```
>E94:@LOOKUP(A96,B96...B109
>B96:0
>C96:0
>A96:@IF((C94<3000),(@INT(C94/25)*25)+12.5,@IF
((C94<50000),(@INT(C94/50)*50)+25,C94)
>B97:3400
>C97:(A96-B97)*.12
>B98:5500
>C98:252+((A96-B98)*.14)
>B99:7600
>C99:546+((A96-B99)*.16)
>B100:11900
>C100:1234+((A96-B100)*.19)
>B101:16000
>C101:2013+((A96-B101)*.22)
>B102:20200
>C102:2937+((A96-B102)*.25)
>B103:24600
>C103:4037+((A96-B103)*.29)
>B104:29900
>C104:5574+((A96-B104)*.33)
>B105:35200
>C105:7323+((A96-B105)*.39)
>B106:45800
>C106:11457+((A96-B106)*.44)
>B107:60000
>C107:17705+((A96-B107)*.49)
>B108:85600
>C108:30249+((A96-B108)*.5)
>B109:1000000000000
>C109:@ERROR
```

User Note: *Range* must evaluate as numbers in ascending order. If *variable* is less than the smallest value in *range* or larger than the greatest value in *range*, @LOOKUP will return the value NA. It is often helpful to place an impossibly low value as the first entry in *range*, and an impossibly high value as the last entry, and associate @ERROR with these entries, to alert the user that *variable* has an unanticipated value.

If *variable* or *cell reference* is less than the smallest value in *range* or greater than the greatest value in source range, the function will return the value NA. It is therefore good practice to give a value in the source range and associated value in the target range for the largest value of *variable*, and to return @ERROR if the source range value is greater than the expected maximum.

@MAX

Syntax: @MAX*(beginrange ... endrange)*
@MAX(element1, *element2, ... elementN)*

Translation: Select the element in the list or range with the highest value.

Problem: Identify the salesperson with the largest average sales for the period and display TRUE opposite that salesperson's sales figure; display FALSE for all others.

Hi-Calc: Salesperson = @MAX(Salesperson1...Salesperson5)

VisiCalc:

	B	C	D	E	F
2	SALESMAN	SALES	SALES	AVERAGE	
3		(DOLLARS)	(UNITS)	($/UNITS)	
4	===				
5	ANDY	123	2	61.50	FALSE
6	BETTY	754	3	251.33	TRUE
7	CHARLES	1032	14	73.71	FALSE
8	DAVID	765	13	58.85	FALSE
9	EDWARD	987	12	82.25	FALSE

>F5:E5 = @MAX(E5.D9)
>F5:/R:F5.F9:RNN

User Note: Values of TRUE, FALSE, NA, or ERROR will cause ERROR to be returned. Labels will evaluate as zero and could be the returned value.

@MIN

Syntax: @MIN*(beginrange...endrange)*
@MIN*(element1, element2,...elementN)*

Translation: Select the element of the list or range with the lowest value.

Problem: Identify the smallest average sale per unit sold, and display TRUE opposite salesperson figure; display FALSE for all others.

Hi-Calc: Salesperson = @MIN (Salesperson1...Salesperson5)

	A	B	C	D	E	F
2		SALESMAN	SALES	SALES	AVERAGE	
3			(DOLLARS)	(UNITS)	($/UNITS)	
4		==				
5		ANDY	123	2	61.50	FALSE
6		BETTY	754	3	251.33	FALSE
7		CHARLES	1032	14	73.71	FALSE
8		DAVID	765	13	58.85	TRUE
9		EDWARD	987	12	82.25	FALSE

>F5:E5 = @MIN(E5.E9)
>F5:/R:F6.F9:RNN

User Note: Values of TRUE, FALSE, NA, or ERROR will cause ERROR to be returned. Labels will evaluate as zero and could be the returned value.

@NA

Syntax: @NA

Translation: Returns the value of NA, that is, not available.

Example: @IF(B2<200,@NA, B2) RETURNS: NA, when value of B2 equals 199.

User Note: Each cell referencing the cell evaluating @NA will as NA. Use @NA when the datum for a particular cell is not yet ready. Also can return NA when a particular condition is tested.

VisiCalc:

	B	C	D	E
2	SALESMAN	SALES	SALES	AVERAGE
3		(DOLLARS)	(UNITS)	($/UNITS)
4	==================================			
5	ANDY	944	NA	NA
6	BETTY	576	7	82.29
7	CHARLES	NA	14	NA
8	DAVID	0	0	0.00
9	EDWARD	754	3	251.33

@NOT

Syntax: @NOT(argument)

Translation: Reverse the Boolean value of argument.

@NOT(@FALSE) = TRUE
@NOT(@TRUE) = FALSE

User Note: A non-Boolean argument will result in a value of ERROR.

@NPV

Syntax: @NPV*(variable, beginrange...endrange)*

Translation: Returns the net present value of the cash flow represented by the range, discounted by the interest rate per time interval, reflected by *variable*.

Problem: Determine the net present value of a bond which pays $63 per year for the next 11 years which returns $1,000 principal plus $63 interest at the end of the 12th year, discounted at a rate of 12 percent.

Hi-Calc: @NPV (.12, 1979 payment.1990 payment)

VisiCalc:

	A	B	C	D
2	DISCOUNT RATE			.12
3				
4		YEAR		RETURN
5		1979		63
6		1980		63
7		1981		63
8		1982		63
9		1983		63
10		1984		63
11		1985		63
12		1986		63
13		1987		63
14		1988		63
15		1989		63
16		1990		1063
17				
18	NET PRES VALUE			646.92

>C18:@NPV(C2,C5...C16)

User Note: *Variable* must be expressed as a decimal fraction rather than as a percentage. Thus a 12 percent annual interest rate would be expressed as .12. If the cash flow reflected in range is at an interval other than annual, *variable* must be adjusted accordingly. Thus, if a range represents a monthly cash flow, a 12 percent annual interest rate would be reflected as ".01".

@OR

Syntax: @OR*(condition1, condition2)*

Translation: Returns TRUE if any one or more of the *conditions* are TRUE, and returns FALSE if each of the *conditions* is FALSE.

Problem: A bonus should be paid if a salesperson's results are over budget on any product.

Hi-Calc: @OR(Budget.Prodone>Sales.Prodone,Budget.Prodtwo>Sale.Prodtwo)

VisiCalc:

	A	B	C	D	E	F	G
2		ANDY		BETTY		CHARLES	
3		SALES	BUDGET	SALES	BUDGET	SALES	BUDGET
4	PROD 1	1010	1000	800	800	1099	1100
5	PROD 2	1450	1400	1350	1120	2000	1540
6		------	------	------	------	------	------
7	TOTAL	2460	2400	2150	1920	3099	2640
		BONUS?	TRUE	BONUS?	TRUE	BONUS?	TRUE

>C9:@OR(B4>C4,B5>C5)
>K9:/R:E9:RRRR
>C9:/R:G9:RRRR

User Note: Will accept multiple Boolean conditions as arguments. If a condition has the value NA, @OR will return NA. Any other value (including a blank, a number, or ERROR) will return ERROR.

@PI

Syntax: @PI

Translation: Returns PI, the number 3.14159266536.

@SIN

Syntax: @SIN*(variable)*

Translation: Returns the sin of angle *variable,* expressed in radians.

Problem: Calculate the value of the tangent of an angle with a given size in radians.

Solution: Sin (1) = 0

	B	C	D	E	F	G
2		57.29578			.0174533	
3	ANGLE	ANGLE	SINE	ANGLE	ANGLE	SINE
4	(RADIANS)	(DEGREES)		(DEGREES)	(RADIANS)	
5	-10	-572.958	.5440211	-90	-1.57080	-1
6	-5	-286.479	.9589243	-45	-.785398	-.707107
7	-1	-57.2958	-.841471	-30	-.523599	-.500000
8	-.5	-28.6479	-.479426	-15	-.261799	-.258819
9	-.25	-14.3239	-.247404	0	0	0
10	0	0	0	30	.5235988	.5000000
11	.25	14.32394	.2474040	60	1.047198	.8660254
12	.5	28.64789	.4794255	75	1.308997	.9659258
13	1	57.29578	.8414710	90	1.570796	1
14	10	572.9578	-.544021	180	3.141593	0

User Note: *Variable* must be expressed in radians. If *variable* is Boolean, @SIN returns ERROR. If *variable* is NA, @SIN returns NA.

@SQRT

Syntax: @SQRT*(variable)*

Translation: Returns the square root of *variable*.

Problem: Calculate the square root of a number.

Solution: @SQRT (25) = 5
@SQRT (−25) = ERROR

User Note: *Variable* must be nonnegative. A Boolean value of *variable* will return ERROR. A label will evaluate to zero and return zero.

@SUM

Syntax: @SUM*(beginrange...endrange)*
@SUM*(element1,element2,...elementN)*

Translation: Returns the arithmetic sum of the range or list.

B: Function Reference Guide

Problem: Calculate the algebraic sum of sales of each salesperson.

Hi-Calc: SALES = (@SUM*(firstsalesperson...lastsalesperson)*

VisiCalc:

	B	C
2	SALESMAN	SALES
3	=================	
4	ANDY	2350
5	BETTY	12500
6	CHARLES	1100
7	DAVID	4700
8	EDWARD	700
9	FRANK	1300
10		-------
11		22650

>C11:@SUM(C4.C9)
>C11:/R:D11.E11:RR

User Note: Arguments may be numbers, individual cell references, or ranges of cell references. Any of these may be combined. A reference to a blank cell or to a label (each of which evaluates to zero) will not disturb the operation of @SUM.

@TAN

Syntax: @TAN*(variable)*

Translation: Returns the tangent of angle of size *variable*, expressed in radians.

Problem: Calculate the tangent of an angle, as measured in radians or in degrees.

	B	C	D	E	F	G
2		57.295779513			.01745329252	
3	ANGLE	ANGLE	TANGENT	ANGLE	ANGLE	TANGENT
4	(RADIANS)	(DEGREES)		(DEGREES)	(RADIANS)	
5	-10	-572.9577951	-0.65	-90	-1.570796327	ERROR
6	-5	-286.4788976	3.38	-45	-.7853981634	-1.00
7	-1	-57.29577951	-1.56	-30	-.5235987756	-0.58
8	-.5	-28.64788976	-0.55	-15	-.2617993878	-0.27
9	-.25	-14.32394488	-0.26	0	0	0.00
10	0	0	0.00	30	.5235987756	0.58
11	.25	14.323944878	0.26	60	1.0471975512	1.73
12	.5	28.647889756	0.55	75	1.308996939	3.73
13	1	57.295779513	1.56	90	1.5707963268	ERROR
14	10	572.95779512	0.65	180	3.1415926536	0.00

User Note: *Variable* must be expressed in radians.

>C2:360/(2*@PI)
>C5:(B5*C2)
>C5:/R:B6.B14:RN
>D5:@TAN(B5)
>D5:/R:D6.D14:R
>F2:(2*@PI)/360
>F5:(E5*F2)
>F5:/R:F6.F14:RN
>G5:@TAN(F5)
>G5:/R:G6.G14:R

@TRUE

Syntax: @TRUE

Translation: Returns the Boolean value TRUE.

APPENDIX C

The Blank Model Template

This appendix consists of the template designed in Chapter 6. The amounts, percents, and other values to be input by the user are indicated by the labels enclosed by the left and right arrows (<>). The inclusion of these labels provides the user with guidance as to which entries the user is to make. This helps to protect the integrity of the formulas and other necessary data entered by the designer. You will note that various cells now contain ERROR, NA, and zero totals due to the lack of data necessary for proper computation of these amounts. When the user completes the data input and recalculates the template, these cells will contain the correct amounts.

```
     A         B         C         D         E         F         G         H         I
 1
 2        A & A PRODUCTS, INC.
 3        1984 FINANCIAL PROJECTIONS
 4
 5     >>>>>>>>>>>>>>>>>>>>>  U S E R    I N P U T  <<<<<<<<<<<<<<<<<<<<<<<<
 6     >                               A N D                                <
 7     >              I N T E R I M   C A L C U L A T I O N S               <
 8     >     ----------------------------------------                       <
 9     >                                                                    <
10     > >> I N P U T   B Y   U S E R <<<<<                                 <
11     >   --------------------------------                                 <
12     >                                                                    <
13     >                                            1984                    <
14     >                                    ----------------------          <
15     > MONTH/SEASON CONVERSION            JAN.    FEB.    MAR.            <
16     > -----------------------           ------  ------  ------           <
17     > MONTH NUMBER                         1       2       3             <
18     > FISCAL QUARTER CODE                  1       1       1             <
19     >                                                                    <
20     >                           BASIS                                    <
21     > SEASONAL FACTORS           CODE  1ST QTR 2ND QTR 3RD QTR 4TH QTR   <
22     > ----------------                 ------- ------- ------- -------   <
23     > LOOKUP CODE                         1       4       7      10      <
24     > SEASON CODE                         1       2       3       4      <
25     > PAYROLL (P/R)       </F$>      1 <RATIO> <RATIO> <RATIO> <RATIO>   <
26     > SALES RELATED(SL    </F$>      2 <RATIO> <RATIO> <RATIO> <RATIO>   <
27     > OTHER [CODE#3]      </F$>      3 <RATIO> <RATIO> <RATIO> <RATIO>   <
28     > SALES, PRODUCT A    </F$>      4 <RATIO> <RATIO> <RATIO> <RATIO>   <
29     > SALES, PRODUCT B    </F$>      5 <RATIO> <RATIO> <RATIO> <RATIO>   <
30     > SALES, PRODUCT C    </F$>      6 <RATIO> <RATIO> <RATIO> <RATIO>   <
31     > MONTHLY INFLTN RATE</F$>< RATE > <RATIO> <RATIO> <RATIO> <RATIO>   <
32     >                                                                    <
33     > PRODUCT MIX:                      JAN.    FEB.    MAR.    TOTAL    <
34     > ------------                     ------  ------  ------  ------    <
35     > PROD-A UNITS                    < UNITS>   0       0       0       <
36     >        SLS PRICE                <  $  >    0       0               <
37     >        COST %                      .7      .7      .7              <
38     > PROD-B UNITS                    < UNITS>   0       0       0       <
39     >        SLS PRICE                <  $  >    0       0               <
40     >        COST %                      .8      .8      .8              <
41     > PROD-C UNITS                    < UNITS>   0       0       0       <
42     >        SLS PRICE                <  $  >    0       0               <
43     >        COST %                      .6      .6      .6              <
44     >                                                                    <
```

C: The Blank Model Template

	A	B	C	D	E	F	G	H	I
45	>				BASIS				<
46	>	OPERATING RATIOS & INPUT			CODE				<
47	>	------------------------			------				<
48	>	SALARIES, OFFICERS			7<	$,000>			<
49	>	SALARIES, OFFICE			10<	$,000>			<
50	>	SALARIES, SALES			1<	$,000>			<
51	>	PAYROLL TAXES			8<	% >			<
52	>	ADVERTISING			2<	% >			<
53	>	BAD DEBT EXPENSE			2<	% >			<
54	>	COMMISSIONS			2<	% >			<
55	>	DELIVERY			2<	% >			<
56	>	DEPRECIATION			9<	$,000>			<
57	>	GROUP INSURANCE			8<	% >			<
58	>	INSURANCE			3<	$,000>			<
59	>	INTEREST			(NOTES)<	% >			<
60	>	LEGAL & ACCOUNTING			7<	$,000>			<
61	>	MOTOR VEHICLE EXPENSE			3<	$,000>			<
62	>	OFFICE SUPPLIES & EXPNS			3<	$,000>			<
63	>	RENT			9<	$,000>			<
64	>	REPAIRS & MAINTENANCE			3<	$,000>			<
65	>	SELLING			2<	% >			<
66	>	TAXES, OTHER			3<	$,000>			<
67	>	TELEPHONE			3<	$,000>			<
68	>	TRADE SHOWS			2<	% >			<
69	>	TRAVEL			2<	% >			<
70	>	INCOME TAXES			(IBIT)<	% >			<
71	>								<
72	>	FINANCIAL RATIOS:							<
73	>	-----------------							<
74	>	INVENTORY DAYS				< DAYS >			<
75	>	CASH DAYS IN OPRTNG EXPS				< DAYS >			<
76	>	ACCOUNTS RECEIVABLE DAYS				< DAYS >			<
77	>	ACCOUNTS PAYABLE DAYS				< DAYS >			<
78	>	ACCRUED EXPENSES DAYS				< DAYS >			<
79	>								<
80	>	OTHER DATA:							<
81	>	-----------							<
82	>	PROPERTY, PLANT & EQUIP.				< $,000>	< $,000>	< $,000>	<
83	>	NOTE PAYABLE ADDITIONS				< $,000>	< $,000>	< $,000>	<
84	>	LONG TERM DEBT ADDITIONS				< $,000>	< $,000>	< $,000>	<
85	>	LONG TERM DEBT REPAYMENTS				< $,000>	< $,000>	< $,000>	<
86	>								<
87	>	>> C O M P U T E D F I E L D S <<<<<<<<							<
88	>								<
89	>	───────────────────────────────────────							<
90	>	TOTAL SALES (000'S)				0	0	0	<
91	>	TOTAL COSTS (000'S)				0	0	0	<
92	>	OVERALL COST %				ERROR	ERROR	ERROR	<
93	>	INVENTORY, ENDING(000'S)<	$,000>			0	0	0	<
94	>	───────────────────────────────────────							<

A	B	C	D	E	F	G	H	I
96				A & A PRODUCTS, INC.				
97			PROJECTED STATEMENT OF INCOME FOR THE YEAR 1984					
98				(000'S)				
99								
100						1984		
101				ACTUAL	------	------	------	------
102				1983	JAN	FEB	MAR	TOTAL
103				------	------	------	------	------
104								
105	SALES			< $,000>	0	0	0	0
106				------	------	------	------	------
107	COST OF SALES:							
108		INVENTORY, BEGINNING		< $,000>	0	0	0	0
109		PURCHASES		< $,000>	0	0	0	0
110				------	------	------	------	------
111				0	0	0	0	0
112		INVENTORY, ENDING		< $,000>	0	0	0	0
113				------	------	------	------	------
114	COST OF SALES			0	0	0	0	0
115				------	------	------	------	------
116	GROSS PROFIT			0	0	0	0	0
117				------	------	------	------	------
118								
119	OPERATING EXPENSES:							
120								
121	SALARIES, OFFICERS			< $,000>	0	0	0	0
122	SALARIES, OFFICE			< $,000>	0	0	0	0
123	SALARIES, SALES			< $,000>	0	0	0	0
124	PAYROLL TAXES			< $,000>	0	0	0	0
125	ADVERTISING			< $,000>	0	0	0	0
126	BAD DEBT EXPENSE			< $,000>	0	0	0	0
127	COMMISSIONS			< $,000>	0	0	0	0
128	DELIVERY			< $,000>	0	0	0	0
129	DEPRECIATION			< $,000>	0	0	0	0
130	GROUP INSURANCE			< $,000>	0	0	0	0
131	INSURANCE			< $,000>	0	0	0	0
132	INTEREST			< $,000>	0	0	0	0
133	LEGAL & ACCOUNTING			< $,000>	0	0	0	0
134	MOTOR VEHICLE EXPENSE			< $,000>	0	0	0	0
135	OFFICE SUPPLIES & EXPNSE			< $,000>	0	0	0	0
136	RENT			< $,000>	0	0	0	0
137	REPAIRS & MAINTENANCE			< $,000>	0	0	0	0
138	SELLING			< $,000>	0	0	0	0
139	TAXES, OTHER			< $,000>	0	0	0	0
140	TELEPHONE			< $,000>	0	0	0	0
141	TRADE SHOWS			< $,000>	0	0	0	0
142	TRAVEL			< $,000>	0	0	0	0
143				------	------	------	------	------
144	OPERATING EXPENSES			0	0	0	0	0
145				------	------	------	------	------
146	INCOME BEFORE INCOME TAX			0	0	0	0	0
147	INCOME TAXES			< $,000>	0	0	0	0
148				------	------	------	------	------
149	NET INCOME			0	0	0	0	0
150				======	======	======	======	======

C: The Blank Model Template

```
    A       B       C       D       E       F       G       H       I
151
152  >>>>>>>>>>>>>>>>>>>>> U S E R    I N P U T <<<<<<<<<<<<<<<<<<<<<<<
153  >                            A N D                                <
154  >             I N T E R I M   C A L C U L A T I O N S             <
155  >                                                                 <
156  >                        ---------------  1984  -----------------
157  >                            1983      ---------------------------
158  >                           ACTUAL    JAN.    FEB.    MAR.        <
159  >                           ------    ------  ------  ------      <
160  > INCOME TAXES PAID                     0       0       0         <
161  > CASH REQUIRED           < $,000>      0       0       0         <
162  > ACCOUNTS RECEIVABLE     < $,000>      0       0       0         <
163  > INVENTORY               < $,000>      0       0       0         <
164  > PREPAID ITEMS  <INPUT>  < $,000>< $,000>< $,000>< $,000>         <
165  > PROPERTY, PLANT & EQUIP.< $,000>      0       0       0         <
166  > OTHER ASSETS   <INPUT>  < $,000>< $,000>< $,000>< $,000>         <
167  > TOTAL ASSETS                 0       0       0       0          <
168  > COMMON STOCK   <INPUT>  < $,000>< $,000>< $,000>< $,000>         <
169  > RETAINED EARNINGS       < $,000>      0       0       0         <
170  > LONG TERM DEBT          < $,000>      0       0       0         <
171  > TOTAL CURRENT LIABS.         0       0       0       0          <
172  > ACCOUNTS PAYABLE        < $,000>      0       0       0         <
173  > ACCRUED EXPENSES        < $,000>      0       0       0         <
174  > INCOME TAXES PAYABLE    < $,000>      0       0       0         <
175  > NOTES PAYABLE           < $,000>      0       0       0         <
176  >_____
```

```
    A       B       C       D       E       F       G       H
177
178                          A & A PRODUCTS, INC.
179                  PROJECTED CASH FLOW FOR THE YEAR 1984
180                               (000'S)
181
182                                          JAN     FEB     MAR
183                                         ------  ------  ------
184    RECEIPTS:
185      CASH, BEGINNING                      0       0       0
186      A/R COLLECTIONS                      0       0       0
187      NOTE ADDITIONS                       0       0       0
188      LONG TERM DEBT                       0       0       0
189                                         ------  ------  ------
190      TOTAL AVAILABLE CASH                 0       0       0
191                                         ------  ------  ------
192    DISBURSEMENTS:
193      PROPERTY,PLANT & EQUIP.              0       0       0
194      ACCOUNTS PAYABLE                     0       0       0
195      ACCRUED EXPENSES                     0       0       0
196      NOTE REPAYMENTS                      0       0       0
197      LONG TERM DEBT                       0       0       0
198      INCOME TAXES                         0       0       0
199                                         ------  ------  ------
200      TOTAL CASH DISBURSED                 0       0       0
209                                         ------  ------  ------
202    CASH, ENDING                           0       0       0
203                                         ======  ======  ======
```

A	B	C	D	E	F	G	H
204							
205		A & A PRODUCTS, INC.					
206	PROJECTED BALANCE SHEETS FOR THE YEAR 1984						
207		(000'S)					
208							
209						1984	
210				ACTUAL	-------	-------	-------
211				1983	JAN	FEB	MAR
212				------	------	------	------
213							
214				ASSETS			
215							
216	CURRENT ASSETS:						
217	CASH			< $,000>	0	0	0
218	ACCOUNTS RECEIVABLE			< $,000>	0	0	0
219	INVENTORY			< $,000>	0	0	0
220	PREPAID ITEMS			< $,000>	0	0	0
221				------	------	------	------
222	TOTAL CURRENT ASSETS			0	0	0	0
223							
224	PROPERTY, PLANT & EQUIP.			< $,000>	0	0	0
225							
226	OTHER ASSETS			< $,000>	0	0	0
227				------	------	------	------
228	TOTAL ASSETS			0	0	0	0
229				======	======	======	======
230							
231		LIABILITIES AND SHAREHOLDERS' EQUITY					
232							
233	CURRENT LIABILITIES:						
234	NOTES PAYABLE			< $,000>	0	0	0
235	ACCOUNTS PAYABLE			< $,000>	0	0	0
236	ACCRUED EXPENSES			< $,000>	0	0	0
237	INCOME TAXES			< $,000>	0	0	0
238				------	------	------	------
239	TOTAL CURRENT						
240	LIABILITIES			0	0	0	0
241				------	------	------	------
242	LONG TERM DEBT			< $,000>	0	0	0
243				------	------	------	------
244	SHAREHOLDERS' EQUITY:						
245	COMMON STOCK			< $,000>	0	0	0
246	RETAINED EARNINGS			< $,000>	0	0	0
247				------	------	------	------
248	TOTAL EQUITY			0	0	0	0
249				------	------	------	------
250	TOTAL LIABILITIES AND						
251	SHAREHOLDERS' EQUITY			0	0	0	0
252				======	======	======	======
253				0	0	0	0
254	DOWNFOOT PROOF						

APPENDIX D

DocuCalc Template Printout

The following printout is another version of the template discussed in Chapter 6. This printout has been generated in a grid format by DocuCalc™, a product of Micro Decision Systems of Pittsburgh, Pa. All labels and numbers have been printed as shown on screen, together with indications of local formatting, if any. Formulas are shown as entered, rather than being evaluated. DocuCalc uses as many lines as is necessary to print a particular formula, locating it within a particular cell.

	A	B	C	D	E	F	G	H	I	J
1										
2		A & A PRODUCTS, INC.								
3		1984 FINANCIAL PROJECTIONS								
4	>>	>>>>>>>>>>>>>>		>>>>> USER A		INPUT <<<<<<	T <<<<<	<<<<<<<	<<<<<<<	<<<<<<<<
5	^			IN	TERI M	NDU	ATIO	N		
6	^	>> INPUT		UT B	Y USE	LCUL		S		
7	^				R <<<<<					
8	^									
9	^									
10	^						1984			
11	^	MONTH/SEASON CON	VERSION		JAN.	FEB.	MAR.		
12	^					1	2	3		
13	^	MONTH NUMBER				1	1	1		
14	^	FISCAL QUARTER C	ODE						
15	^									
16	^			BASIS						
17	^	SEASONAL FACTORS		CODE	1ST QTR	2ND QTR	3RD QTR	4TH QTR	
18	^	LOOKUP CODE	</F$>	1	1	4	7	10	
19	^	SEASON CODE	</F$>	2	1	2	3	4	
20	^	PAYROLL (P/R)	</F$>	3	1.03	.97	.99	1.1	
21	^	SALES RELATED(SLODE@3]	</F$>	4	1.07	1.02	.97	.99	
22	^	OTHER [CODE@3]	</F$>	4	1.03	1.01	.97	.95	
23	^	SALES, PRODUCT A	</F$>	5	1.1	1.15	1.08	1.1	
24	^	SALES, PRODUCT B	</F$>	6	.98	.94	.99	.95	
25	^	SALES, PRODUCT C	</F$>	1	1.07	1.12	.99	.96	
26	^	MONTHLY INFLTN RATE</F$>							
27	^									
28	^	PRODUCT MIX:			JAN.	FEB.	MAR.	TOTAL	
29	^	PROD-A UNITS			10000	(@INT((+F3 5*@CHOOSE(G18,F28... I28))+.5)	(@INT((+G3 5*@CHOOSE(H18,F28... I28))+.5)	@INT(F36*(E31^(H17-1))+.5)	@SUM(F35..H35)
33										
34										
35										
36	^	S	LS PRICE		40	@INT(F36*(E31^(G17-1))+.5)			
37	^	C	OST %		@IF(F35<11 001,.7,@IF (F35<12001 ,.685,@IF(F35<13001, -.675,.67))	@IF(G35<11 001,.7,@IF (G35<12001 ,.685,@IF(G35<13001, -.675,.67))	@IF(H35<11 001,.7,@IF (H35<12001 ,.685,@IF(H35<13001, -.675,.67))		
38	^	PROD-B UNITS			20000	(@INT((+F3 8*@CHOOSE(G18,F29... I29))+.5)	(@INT((+G3 8*@CHOOSE(H18,F29... I29))+.5)	@INT(F39*(E31^(H17-1))+.5)	@SUM(F38..H38)
39	^	S	LS PRICE		36	@INT(F39*(			

D: DocuCalc Template Printout

Row	A	B	C	D	E	F	G	H	I	J
40	>		C OST %		<FRMULA>	@IF(F38<20 001,.8,@IF (F38<21501 ,.78,@IF(F 38<23001,. 765,.755))	@IF(F38<20 001,.8,@IF (G38<21501 ,.78,@IF(G 38<23001,. 765,.755))	E31^(G17-1)+.5) @IF(H38<20 001,.8,@IF (H38<21501 ,.78,@IF(H 38<23001,. 765,.755))	E31^(H17-1)+.5)	v
41	>	PROD-C U NITS				100000		(@INT((+F4 1*@CHOOSE(G18,F30... H18,F30... I30))+.5)	(@INT((+G4 1*@CHOOSE(1*@CHOOSE(.H41)	v
42	>		S LS PRICE			3			@SUM(F41..	v
43	>		C OST %		<FRMULA>	@IF(F41<10 001,.6,@IF 01,.59,@IF (F41<10800 1,,575,.56 5))	@IF(G41<10 001,.6,@IF F(G41<1050 01,.59,@IF (G41<10800 1,,575,.56 5))	@IF(H41<10 001,.6,@IF F(H41<1050 01,.59,@IF (H41<10800 1,,575,.56 5))	E31^(H17-1)+.5) @IF(F42*(E31^(G17-1 @IF(F42*( )+.5)	v
44	^				BASIS					v
45	^	OPERATIN	G RATIOS	& INPUT	CODE					v
46	^	--------	--------	--------	----					v
47	^			RS						v
48	^	SALARIES	, OFFICE		7	24				v
49	^	SALARIES	, OFFICE		10	30				v
50	^	SALARIES	, SALES		1	20				v
51	^	PAYROLL	TAXES		8	.08				v
52	^	ADVERTIS	ING		2	.015				v
53	^	BAD DEBT	EXPENSE		2	.015				v
54	^	COMMISSI	ONS		2	.03				v
55	^	DELIVERY			2	.014				v
56	^	DEPRECIA	TION		9	9				v
57	^	GROUP IN	SURANCE		8	.08				v
58	^	INSURANC	E		3	8				v
59	^	INTEREST		(NOTES)		.15				v
60	^	LEGAL &	ACCOUNTI	NG	3	5				v
61	^	MOTOR VE	HICLE EX	PENSE	3	4				v
62	^	OFFICE S	UPPLIES	& EXPNS	9	4				v
63	^	RENT			3	5				v
64	^	REPAIRS	& MAINTE	NANCE	3	5				v
65	^	SELLING			2	.008				v
66	^	TAXES, O	THER		3	2				v
67	^	TELEPHON	E		3	3				v
68	^	TRADE SH	OWS		2	.003				v
69	^	TRAVEL			2	.004				v
70	^	INCOME T	AXES	(IBIT)		.44				v
71	^									v
72	^	FINANCIA	L RATIOS	::						v
73	^	--------	--------	-						v
74	^	INVENTOR	Y DAYS			28				v

	A	B	C	D	E	F	G	H	I	J
75	>	CASH DAYS IN OPR		TNG EXPS		60				v
76	>	ACCOUNTS RECEIVABLE DAYS				45				v
77	>	ACCOUNTS PAYABLE DAYS				35				v
78	>	ACCRUED EXPENSES DAYS				30				v
79	>									v
80	>	OTHER DATA:								v
81	>	PROPERTY, PLANT & EQUIP.				10	10	10		v
82	>	NOTE PAYABLE ADDITIONS				0	0	0		v
83	>	LONG TERM DEBT ADDITIONS				0	0	0		v
84	>	LONG TERM DEBT REPAYMENT				3	3	3		v
85	>									v
86	>									v
87	>	>> COMPUTED FIELDS				<<<<<<<				v
88	>									
89	>									v
90		TOTAL SALES (000'S)				(@INT(((F3 5*F36)+(F3 8*F39)+(F4 1*F42)/100 0)+.5)	(@INT(((G3 5*G36)+(G3 8*G39)+(G4 1*G42)/100 0)+.5)	(@INT(((H3 5*H36)+(H3 8*H39)+(H4 1*H42)/100 0)+.5)		v
91	>	TOTAL COSTS (000'S)				(@INT(((F3 5*F36*F37) +(F38*F39* F40)+(F41* F42*F43)/1 000)+.5)	(@INT(((G3 5*G36*G37) +(G38*G39* G40)+(G41* G42*G43)/1 000)+.5)	(@INT(((H3 5*H36*H37) +(H38*H39* H40)+(H41* H42*H43)/1 000)+.5)		
92	>	OVERALL COST %				(@INT(+F9 1/30*F74)+ .5)	(@INT(+G9 1/30*F74)+ .5)	(@INT(+H9 1/30*F74)+ .5)		
93	>	INVENTORY, ENDING (000'S)			945	+F91/F90	+G91/G90	+H91/H90		
94	>									
95			PRI		& A PROD	UCTS, IN	C.			
96				PROJECTED STATEMENT OF INCOME FOR THE YEAR 1984						
97					(000'S)					
98										
99					ACTUAL 1983	JAN	FEB	MAR	TOTAL	
100										
101										
102										
103										
104										
105		SALES			15550	+F90	+G90	+H90	@SUM(F105..H105)	
106		COST OF SALES:								
107		INVENTORY, BEGINNING			875	+E112	+F112	+G112	+E108	
108		PURCHASES			12443	+F91+F93-F 108	+G91+G93-G 108	+H91+H93-H 108	@SUM(F109..H109)	
109					+E108+E109	@SUM(F108..F110)	@SUM(G108..G110)	@SUM(H108..H110)	@SUM(F110..H110)	
110										
111		INVENTORY, ENDING			945	+F93	+G93	+H93	@SUM(F111..H111)	
112									.-H112	
113		COST OF SALES			+E111-E112	+F111-F112	+G111-G112	+H111-H112	@SUM(F114..	
114										

170 APPENDIXES

D: DocuCalc Template Printout

A	B	C	D	E	F	G	H	I	J
115									
116	GROSS PR	OFIT		+E105-E114	+F105-F114	+G105-G114	+H105-H114	@SUM(F16..H116	..H114
117				---------	---------	---------	---------	---------	
118									
119	OPERATIN	G EXPENS	ES:						
120									
121	SALARIES	, OFFICE	RS	250	+F48	@IF(@AND(E31>1.02,@SUM(F149...G17<10),@INT(F121-(E31^(G17-1))+.5)+100*(E31^(G17-1))+.5)	@IF(@AND(E31>1.02,@SUM(F149...UM(F149...G149)>2250,H17<10),@INT(F121-(E31^(H17-1))+.5)+100*(E31^(H17-1))+.5)	@SUM(F121..H121)
122	SALARIES	, OFFICE		342	@INT((+F49*(E31^(F17-1))+.5)	@INT(+F49*(E31^(G17-1))+.5)	@INT(+F49*(E31^(H17-1))+.5)	@SUM(F122..H122)
123	SALARIES	, SALES		165	+F50	@INT((F12 3*E31*(@IF(E50=1,@CHOOSE(G18,F OOSE(G18,F 25...I25), @IF(E50=2,@CHOOSE(H1 8,F26...I2 6),@CHOOSE(G18,F27...I27)))+.5))	@INT((@IF(G12 3*E31*(@IF (E50=1,@CH OOSE(H18,F 25...I25), @IF(E50=2,@CHOOSE(H1 8,F26...I2 6),@CHOOSE(H18,F27...I27)))+.5)	@SUM(F123..H123)
124	PAYROLL	TAXES		60	(@INT((@SU M(F121...F 123)*F51)+.5))	(@INT((@SU M(G121...G M(H121...H 123)*F51)+.5))	(@INT((@SU M(H121...H 123)*F51)+.5))	@SUM(F124..H124)
125	ADVERTIS	ING		131	(@INT((+F5 2*F105))+.5)	(@INT((F12 5*E31*(@IF (E52=1,@CH OOSE(G18,F 25...I25), @IF(E52=2,@CHOOSE(G1 8,F26...I2 6),@CHOOSE(G18,F27...I27)))+.5))	(@INT((G12 5*E31*(@IF (E52=1,@CH OOSE(H18,F 25...I25), @IF(E52=2,@CHOOSE(H1 8,F26...I2 6),@CHOOSE(H18,F27...I27)))+.5)	@SUM(F125..H125)
126	BAD DEBT	EXPENSE		165	(@INT((+F5 3*F105)+.5))	(@INT((F12 6*E31*(@IF (E53=1,@CH OOSE(G18,F OOSE(G18,F	(@INT((G12 6*E31*(@IF (E53=1,@CH OOSE(H18,F	@SUM(F126..H126)

171

	A	B	C	D	E	F	G	H	I	J
127		COMMISSI	ONS		443	(@INT((+F5 4*F105)+.5))	(@INT((F12 7*E31*(@IF (E54=1,@CH OOSE(G18,F 25...I25), @IF(E54=2, @CHOOSE(H1 8,F26...I2 6),@CHOOSE (G18,F27.. .I27)))+. 5))	(@INT((F12 7*E31*(@IF (E54=1,@CH OOSE(H18,F 25...I25), @IF(E54=2, @CHOOSE(H1 8,F26...I2 6),@CHOOSE (G18,F27.. .I27)))+. 5))	@SUM(F127 ..H127)
128		DELIVERY			187	(@INT((+F5 5*F105)+.5))	(@INT((F12 8*E31*(@IF (E55=1,@CH OOSE(G18,F 25...I25), @IF(E55=2, @CHOOSE(H1 8,F26...I2 6),@CHOOSE (G18,F27.. .I27)))+. 5))	(@INT((F12 8*E31*(@IF (E55=1,@CH OOSE(H18,F 25...I25), @IF(E55=2, @CHOOSE(H1 8,F26...I2 6),@CHOOSE (G18,F27.. .I27)))+. 5))	@SUM(F128 ..H128)
129		DEPRECIA	TION		76	+F56	+F56	+F56	@SUM(F129 ..H129)
130		GROUP IN	SURANCE		65	(@INT((@SU M(F121...G 123)*F57)+ .5))	(@INT((@SU M(G121...G 123)*F57)+ .5))	(@INT((@SU M(H121...H 123)*F57)+ .5))	@SUM(F130 ..H130)
131		INSURANC	E		67	+F58	(@INT((G13 1*E31*(@IF (E58=1,@CH OOSE(G18,F 25...I25), @IF(E58=2, @CHOOSE(H1 8,F26...I2 6),@CHOOSE (G18,F27.. .I27)))+. 5))	(@INT((G13 1*E31*(@IF (E58=1,@CH OOSE(H18,F 25...I25), @IF(E58=2, @CHOOSE(H1 8,F26...I2 6),@CHOOSE (G18,F27.. .I27)))+. 5))	@SUM(F131 ..H131)
132		INTEREST			87	(@INT((F59 /12*E234)+ .5))	(@INT((F59 /12*F234)+ .5))	(@INT((F59 /12*G234)+ .5))	@SUM(F132 ..H132)
133		LEGAL &	ACCOUNTI	NG	46	+F60	@INT(F133* .5))	@INT(F133* .5))	@SUM(F133

D: DocuCalc Template Printout

A	B	C	D	E	F	G	H	I	J
134		MOTOR VE	HICLE EX PENSE	41	+F61	(E31^(G17-1))+.5)	(E31^(H17-1))+.5)	(@INT((F13 4*E31*(@IF (E61=1,@CH OOSE(G18,F 25..I25), @IF(E61=2, @CHOOSE(G1 8,F26..I2 6),@CHOOSE (G18,F27.. .I27)))+. 5))	@SUM(F134 ..H134)
135		OFFICE S	UPPLIES & EXPNSE	37	+F62	(@INT((F13 5*E31*(@IF (E62=1,@CH OOSE(G18,F 25..I25), @IF(E62=2, @CHOOSE(G1 8,F26..I2 6),@CHOOSE (G18,F27.. .I27)))+. 5))	(@INT((G13 5*E31*(@IF (E62=1,@CH OOSE(H18,F 25..I25), @IF(E62=2, @CHOOSE(H1 8,F26..I2 6),@CHOOSE (H18,F27.. .I27)))+. 5))	@SUM(F135 ..H135)
136		RENT		48	+F63				@SUM(F136 ..H136)
137		REPAIRS	& MAINTE NANCE	51	+F64	(@INT((F13 7*E31*(@IF (E64=1,@CH OOSE(G18,F 25..I25), @IF(E64=2, @CHOOSE(G1 8,F26..I2 6),@CHOOSE (G18,F27.. .I27)))+. 5))	(@INT((G13 7*E31*(@IF (E64=1,@CH OOSE(H18,F 25..I25), @IF(E64=2, @CHOOSE(H1 8,F26..I2 6),@CHOOSE (H18,F27.. .I27)))+. 5))	@SUM(F137 ..H137)
138		SELLING		106	(@INT((+F6 5*F105)+.5))	(@INT((F13 8*E31*(@IF (E65=1,@CH OOSE(G18,F 25..I25), @IF(E65=2, @CHOOSE(G1 8,F26..I2 6),@CHOOSE (G18,F27.. .I27)))+. 5))	(@INT((F13 8*E31*(@IF (E65=1,@CH OOSE(H18,F 25..I25), @IF(E65=2, @CHOOSE(H1 8,F26..I2 6),@CHOOSE (H18,F27.. .I27)))+. 5))	@SUM(F138 ..H138)
139		TAXES, O	THER	15	+F66	+F66	+F66		@SUM(F139 ..H139)

	A	B	C	D	E	F	G	H	I	J
140		TELEPHONE			30	+F67	(@INT((F14 0*E31*(@IF (E67=1,@CH OOSE(G18,F 25..I25), @IF(E67=2, @CHOOSE(G1 8,F26..I2 6),@CHOOSE (G18,F27.. .I27)))+. 5))	(@INT((G14 0*E31*(@IF (E67=1,@CH OOSE(H18,F 25..I25), @IF(E67=2, @CHOOSE(H1 8,F26..I2 6),@CHOOSE (H18,F27.. .I27)))+. 5))	@SUM(F140. .H140)	
141		TRADE SHOWS			18	(@INT((+F6 8*F105)+.5))	(@INT((F14 1*E31*(@IF (E68=1,@CH OOSE(G18,F 25..I25), @IF(E68=2, @CHOOSE(G1 8,F26..I2 6),@CHOOSE (G18,F27.. .I27)))+. 5))	(@INT((F14 1*E31*(@IF (E68=1,@CH OOSE(H18,F 25..I25), @IF(E68=2, @CHOOSE(H1 8,F26..I2 6),@CHOOSE (H18,F27.. .I27)))+. 5))	@SUM(F141. .H141)	
142		TRAVEL			60	(@INT((+F6 9*F105)+.5))	(@INT((F14 2*E31*(@IF (E69=1,@CH OOSE(G18,F 25..I25), @IF(E69=2, @CHOOSE(G1 8,F26..I2 6),@CHOOSE (G18,F27.. .I27)))+. 5))	(@INT((F14 2*E31*(@IF (E69=1,@CH OOSE(H18,F 25..I25), @IF(E69=2, @CHOOSE(H1 8,F26..I2 6),@CHOOSE (H18,F27.. .I27)))+. 5))	@SUM(F142. .H142)	
143					========					
144		OPERATING EXPENSES			@SUM(E121. .E143)	@SUM(F121. .F143)	@SUM(G121. .G143)	@SUM(H121. .H143)	@SUM(F144. .H144)	
145					========					
146		INCOME BEFORE INCOME TAX			+E116-E144	+F116-F144	+G116-G144	+H116-H144	@SUM(F146. .H146)	
147		INCOME TAXES			287	(@INT((F70 *F146)+.5)	(@INT((F70 *G146)+.5)	(@INT((F70 *H146)+.5)	@SUM(F147. .H147)	
148										
149		NET INCOME			+E146-E147	+F146-F147	+G146-G147	+H146-H147	@SUM(F149. .H149)	
150	>>>>>>>>>	>>>>>>>>	>>>>>>>>	>>>>> U	S E R	I N P U	T <<<<<	<<<<<<<	<<<<<<<<	<<<<<
151	^									
152	^			I N	T E R	A	N D	C A		
153	^				M C	A	L C U L	A T I O	N S	
154	^				----			----		
155	^						1984			
156										

D: DocuCalc Template Printout

	A	B	C	D	E	F	G	H	I	J
					1983	JAN.	FEB.	MAR.		
					ACTUAL					
157	>		INCOME TAXES PAID	D		@IF(@OR(F147=4,F17=6,F17=9,G17=12),@INT((E147/4)+.5),@IF(F17=3,+E237,0)	@IF(@OR(G17=4,G17=6,G17=9,G17=12),@INT((E147/4)+.5),@IF(G17=3,+E237,0)	@IF(@OR(H17=4,H17=6,H17=9,H17=12),@INT((E147/4)+.5),@IF(H17=3,+E237,0)	>
158	>									
159	>									
160	>									
161	>	CASH REQUIRED			321	(@INT(((F144-F129)/30*F75)+.5)	(@INT(((G144-G129)/30*F75)+.5)	(@INT(((H144-H129)/30*F75)+.5)	>
162	>	ACCOUNTS RECEIVABLE	BLE		2167	(@INT(F105/30*F76)+.5)	(@INT(G105/30*F76)+.5)	(@INT(H105/30*F76)+.5)	>
163	>	INVENTORY ITEMS	<INPUT>		945	+F112	+G112	+H112	>
164	>	PREPAID, PLANT	& EQUIP.		132	132	132	132	>
165	>	PROPERTY			437	+F224+F82-F129	+F224+G82-G129	+G224+H82-H129	>
166	>	OTHER ASSETS	<INPUT>		76	76	76	76	>
167	>	TOTAL ASSETS			@SUM(E161..E166)	@SUM(F161..F166)	@SUM(G161..G166)	@SUM(H161..H166)	>
168	>	COMMON STOCK	<INPUT>		300	300	300	300	>
169	>	RETAINED EARNINGS	S		1259	+E246+F149	+F246+G149	+G246+H149	>
170	>	LONG TERM DEBT			180	+E242+F84-F85	+F242+G84-G85	+G242+H84-H85	>
171	>	TOTAL CURRENT LIABS.			+E167-@SUM(E168...E170)	+F167-@SUM(F168...G170)	+G167-@SUM(G168...G170)	+H167-@SUM(H168...H170)	>
172	>	ACCOUNTS PAYABLE			943	(@INT((F10 9/30*F77)+.5)	(@INT((G10 9/30*F77)+.5)	(@INT((H10 9/30*F77)+.5)	>
173	>	ACCRUED EXPENSES			256	(@INT(((F144-F121-F22-F123-F129)/30*F78)+.5)+E237+F147-F160	(@INT(((G144-G121-G22-G123-G129)/30*F78)+.5)+F237+G147-G160	(@INT(((H144-H121-H22-H123-H129)/30*F78)+.5)+G237+H147-H160	>
174	>	INCOME TAXES PAYABLE			40	+F171-@SUM(F172...F174)	+G171-@SUM(G172...G174)	+H171-@SUM(H172...H174)	>
175	>	NOTES PAYABLE			1100				>
176	>¦								¦
177				A & A PRODUCTS,	INC.				
178			PRI PROJECTED	CASH F LOW FOR	THE YEAR	1984			
179				(0 00'S)					
180									
181						JAN	FEB	MAR	
182									
183		RECEIPTS:							
184									

A	B	C	D	E	F	G	H	I	J
185	CASH, B	EGINNING			+E217	+F202	+G202		
186	A/R COL	LECTIONS			+E218+F105	+F218+G105	+G218+H105		
187	NOTE AD	DITIONS			-F162	-G162	-H162		
188	LONG TE	RM DEBT			+F83	+G83	+H83		
189					+F84	+G84	+H84		
190	TOTAL	AVAILABL	E CASH		@SUM(F185..F189)	@SUM(G185..G189)	@SUM(H185..H189)		
191	DISBURSE	MENTS:							
192	PROPERT	Y,PLANT	& EQUIP.		+F82	+G82	+H82		
193	ACCOUNT	S PAYABL	E		+E235+F109	+F235+G109	+G235+H109		
194					-F172	-G172	-H172		
195	ACCRUED	EXPENSE	S		+E236+F144 -F129-F173	+F236+G144 -G129-G173	+G236+H144 -H129-H173		
196	NOTE RE	PAYMENTS			+E234+F187 -F175	+F234+G187 -G175	+G234+H187 -H175		
197	LONG TE	RM DEBT			+F85	+G85	+H85		
198	INCOME	TAXES			+F160	+G160	+H160		
199									
200	TOTAL	CASH DIS	BURSED		@SUM(F193..F199)	@SUM(G193..G199)	@SUM(H193..H199)		
201	CASH, EN	DING			+F190-F200	+G190-G200	+H190-H200		
202									
203									
204									
205			PRI						
206		PRO	JECTED B	A & A PRO	ODUCTS,				
207				ALANCE S	HEETS FO				
208					(0	00'S)			
209									
210					ACTUAL		1984		
211					1983	JAN	FEB	MAR	
212									
213				ASSETS					
214									
215		CURRENT	ASSETS:						
216		CASH			321	+F202	+G202	+H202	
217		ACCOUNT	S RECEIV	ABLE	2167	+F162	+G162	+H162	
218		INVENTO	RY		945	+F112	+G112	+H112	
219		PREPAID	ITEMS		132	+F164	+G164	+H164	
220									
221		TOTAL CUR	RRENT AS	SETS	@SUM(E216..E221)	@SUM(F216..F221)	@SUM(G216..G221)	@SUM(H216..H221)	
222									
223		PROPERTY	, PLANT	& EQUIP.	437	+E224+F193 -F129	+F224+G193 -G129	+G224+H193 -H129	
224									
225									
226		OTHER AS	SETS		76	+F166	+G166	+H166	
227									
228		TOTAL AS	SETS		@SUM(E222..E227)	@SUM(F222..F227)	@SUM(G222..G227)	@SUM(H222..H227)	
229					======	======	======	======	

D: DocuCalc Template Printout

	A	B	C	D	E	F	G	H	I
230			LIABILIT	IES AND	SHAREHOL	DERS' EQ	UITY		
231									
232		CURRENT	LIABILIT	IES:					
233		NOTES P	AYABLE		1100	+F175	+G175	+H175	
234		ACCOUNT	S PAYABL	E	943	+F172	+G172	+H172	
235		ACCRUED	EXPENSE	S	256	+F173	+G173	+H173	
236		INCOME	TAXES		40	+F174	+G174	+H174	
237					------	------	------	------	
238		TOTAL CU	RRENT		@SUM(E234..E238)	@SUM(F234..F238)	@SUM(G234..G238)	@SUM(H234..H238)	
239			LIABI LITIES						
240		LONG TER	M DEBT		180	+F170	+G170	+H170	
241									
242		SHAREHOL	DERS' EQ	UITY:					
243									
244		COMMON	STOCK		300	+F168	+G168	+H168	
245		RETAINE	D EARNIN	GS	1259	+F169	+G169	+H169	
246					------	------	------	------	
247		TOTAL EQ	UITY		+E245+E246	@SUM(F245..F247)	@SUM(G245..G247)	@SUM(H245..H247)	
248									
249		TOTAL LI	ABILITIE	S AND					
250		SHAREH	OLDERS'	EQUITY	+E240+E242 +E248	+F240+F242 +F248	+G240+G242 +G248	+H240+H242 +H248	
251					======	======	======	======	
252									
253	DOWNFOOT	PROOF			+E228-E251	+F228-F251	+G228-G251	+H228-H251	

GLOSSARY

Argument: A Boolean or mathematical expression, e.g., a number, variable, or value resulting from a formula, which is used by a Boolean or mathematical function in further calculations. In VisiCalc, an argument may be a number, a formula, or a cell reference. For example, the sum of the contents of Cells C4 through C9, expressed by the formula "@SUM(C4...C9)", contains the function @SUM and the argument C4...C9, which represents the range of cells upon which the function is to operate. In the formula @LOOKUP(G15, B5...B10), the cell reference G15 as well as the range B5...B10 are arguments to the @LOOKUP function.

ASCII: American Standard Code for Information Interchange. A computer coding scheme used to represent a total of 128 letters and other symbols by combinations of 16 pieces of information. Almost all personal computers use ASCII codes.

Backup: Copies of programs or data files for use in the event the original files are lost.

Blank: To erase the contents of a cell, including data and local formats.

Boolean: Related to the logical value of TRUE or FALSE. A Boolean expression may evaluate as either TRUE or FALSE, depending on the values in these cells. The values in a Boolean expression in a VisiCalc worksheet may consist of complex formulas and/or references to other cells containing values or formulas.

Bug: An error, particularly in template logic or design.

Carriage Return: An instruction given to the monitor screen or printer to return the cursor or printhead to the leftmost horizontal position. A Control-M (or hexagonal value 0C) is commonly understood as a carriage return instruction. Many printers and computers automatically execute a linefeed after a carriage return, so that the cursor or printhead moves to the next line at the same time it returns to the leftmost horizontal position.

Cell: A location on a VisiCalc worksheet denoted by the coordinates of an intersection of a column and a row, i.e., Cell B4 is the cell located in Column B on Row 4. All labels, data, and formulas are entered into cells.

Circular Reference: Formed when two cells contain formulas that refer to each other. Circular references may occasionally be used intentionally, but most often lead to inaccurate results.

Column: In VisiCalc, a group of 254 adjacent cells arranged in a vertical line. VisiCalc columns are named with the letters A to BK.

Commands: The built-in features of VisiCalc which enable a VisiCalc user to instruct the program to perform a defined set of procedures. (See Appendix A for an explanation of VisiCalc's commands).

Control Key: The key on the computer's keyboard identified as CTRL or some similar abbreviation. When depressed at the same time as another key, the meaning of the second key is altered. This second meaning usually instructs the computer or some peripheral to do something. Many of the sets of ASCII characters require the control key to be entered.

Coordinate: The identification of the intersection point of a column and a row on a VisiCalc worksheet. This may also be thought of as the "name" of a cell.

Cursor: The location on the monitor screen where the next entry will be made. Depending on the computer and the program, the cursor may be indicated by inverse video (light background and dark characters), by flashing, or by some other method.

Cursor Cell: The current position of the VisiCalc cursor. The cell where the next VisiCalc entry will be made, usually indicated in inverse video (light background with dark characters). The cursor cell, and its contents, is shown on the VisiCalc entry line.

Data: Labels, formulas, or mathematical values to be entered into or computed by VisiCalc.

Debug: The process of finding and removing errors in template or program design or logic.

DIF: Data Interchange Format is a standardized data file storage format originated by Software Arts, Inc. Labels and numeric values stored in DIF by VisiCalc can be used by other programs; DIF files generated by other programs can be used by VisiCalc. DIF may also be used to move data from one location to another in the same VisiCalc template. DIF files may be saved using the /S#S command, and reloaded into a template using the /S#L command.

Disk: An offline storage medium for storage of computer data or programs.

Expression: A group of characters which represents an arithmetic or Boolean operation or idea.

File: A collection of information which may be saved to disk and retrieved from disk. Files are usually named when they are saved, and may be retrieved by use of the same name. A file may contain instructions for a computer to execute programs or data.

Floppy Disk: A plastic magnetically coated offline storage medium for moderate speed storage of hundreds of thousands of information characters. Most floppy disks are either 8 inches or 5¼ inches in diameter, and rotate at approximately 300 revolutions per minute.

Glossary

Format: The manner in which the information in a cell is displayed. Formats may be altered by using the /F or /GF commands. A format does not affect the actual value retained in the cell that is used by VisiCalc for further calculations.

Forward Reference: The entry into a cell (entry cell) of a formula which includes the coordinates of another cell (referenced cell) which may also contain a formula and is evaluated prior to the entry cell. This can lead to inaccurate results unless multiple recalculations are made. A forward reference does not present a problem if the referenced cell contains only values and not formulas.

Function: A mathematical or Boolean rule for manipulation of data. VisiCalc has a number of built-in functions such as @SUM, @NPV, and @IF.

Global: A command affecting all cells, or coordinate locations, on a VisiCalc worksheet. Global commands affect format, column width, automatic or manual recalculation, and order of recalculation by row or by column.

Global Format: A format affecting all cells on a template not set to a specific local format. Global formats may be altered by using the /GF command.

Hard Disk: An offline storage medium for high-speed storage of millions of information characters. Within current technology, specially treated platters spin in evacuated chambers at a rate of more than 3,000 revolutions per minute.

Hexadecimal: Number system to base 16. Digits used are 0, 1, 2, 3, 4, 5, 6, 7, 8, 9, A, B, C, D, E, F.

Input: Data or other information directed to the computer, usually from a disk or the keyboard.

Internal Rate of Return (IRR): That particular interest rate at which the net present value of an income stream is equal to the required present investment. IRR is a commonly used, although imperfect, measure of an investment's value.

Label: An alphanumeric entry in a VisiCalc cell which is intended not to represent a mathematical value but is, in effect, the name of something. If, within a formula, reference is made to a cell containing a label, it will be evaluated as a zero.

Linefeed: An instruction given to the monitor screen (CRT) or printer to increment the current line position. A Control-J (or hexadecimal value 0A) is commonly understood as a linefeed instruction.

List: A group of cells upon which a function can operate. A list can include a range of adjacent cells, i.e., B10...B30, or simply a statement of the included cells, i.e., B2, C5, F4...F7, E17, BK254.

Load: To retrieve a program or data from offline storage media, particularly disks. VisiCalc templates may be loaded using the /SL command.

Local Format: A format affecting only one cell. Local formats may be set by using the /F command, and will override conflicting global formats.

Modem: MODulator/DEModulator. A device used to enable a computer to communicate with other computers, particularly over telephone lines.

Net Present Value: The current value of a future stream of income discounted by a given interest rate. VisiCalc will calculate a net present value using the @NPV function.

Order of Recalculation: The direction in which calculations are made by VisiCalc, i.e., down the columns, a column at a time, or across the rows, a row at a time.

Output: Data or other information directed from the computer, usually to a disk, a printer, or another computer.

Overlay: The process of loading VisiCalc data (labels, formulas, and values) from a previously saved file over an existing worksheet currently in RAM. Unintended overlays may occur if the memory is not cleared using the /CY command prior to loading a new file.

Pound: To replace a formula presently contained within a cell with the value resulting from that formula. This is done by placing the cursor in the desired cell, pressing the [#] key, and then pressing **[RETURN]**.

Projections: An estimate of future financial results.

RAM: Random Access Memory more accurately described as Read/Write memory. This is the volatile workspace in the computer where programs operate upon and create data. Data and programs in RAM are usually lost when the computer is turned off or a power failure occurs.

Range: A list of adjacent cells in the same column or row. A range can be represented by the beginning and ending coordinates of the series which must be separated by a "." when entered. VisiCalc displays the beginning and ending cells of a range separated by ". . .". For example, "B4. B10" or "B4. . .B10" is equivalent to "B4, B5, B6, B7, B8, B9, B10".

Recursive: Description of a formula that uses itself as an argument. See recursive.

Report: A rectangular area of a VisiCalc template containing the results of the calculations in the template, usually designed to be printed.

Roll: To prepare a template containing financial reports for the next reporting period by relocating the current period's final totals as the next period's previous totals.

ROM: Read Only Memory. ROM is used to store programs and data which are available to the computer without being read in from a disk. Data and programs stored in ROM are not lost when the computer is turned off or a power failure occurs.

Row: A group of 63 adjacent cells arranged in a horizontal line. VisiCalc rows are named with the numbers 1 through 254.

Save: To store programs or data onto offline storage media, particularly disks. VisiCalc templates are saved using the /SS command.

Setup String: One or more characters sent to a printer to select printer options such as character size and maximum line length.

Software: Computer instruction stored on offline storage media, particularly disks, which tell the computer what to do.

Source Range: A range of cells to be replicated (copied) to another space on the VisiCalc worksheet (called the target range).

Target Range: A range of cells to which a source range of cells will be replicated.

Template: For those who dislike accounting jargon, a synonym for "worksheet."

Textfile: A file containing information which may be interpreted as plain-language text.

Tuple: A section of a DIF file representing values taken from adjacent VisiCalc cells.

Value: A number that is the result of a mathematical formula or a Boolean expression (TRUE or FALSE). Labels are evaluated as a zero.

Variable: A reference in a formula to a value contained in another cell.

Vector: A particular value within a DIF file tuple.

VisEXEC: VisiCalc instructions stored on disk which are executed, as if they were entered manually from the keyboard, by VisiCalc as they are read into the computer with a /SL command.

Word Processor: A program which enables a computer operator to create and manipulate textfiles, particularly for letters, books, and similar documents. Also, a single purpose computer used for word processing purposes, particularly by an office secretary.

Worksheet: For those with an aversion to engineering jargon, a synonym for "template." Also, a piece of paper containing columns and rows.

INDEX

A

@ABS, 141–42
Accountant's worksheet, 5–6
Accounting equation, 82–83
Accounts receivable formula, 96
ACCUM.PRF file, 67–72
Accumulating, 67–72
@ACOS, 142
/AL labels with gutters, 114
@AND, 51
Apple Computer, Inc., Profile, 102
Apple 16K expansion board, 79
Apple II, 2, 20, 24, 73, 77–78, 79–88
Apple IIe, 79–80
Apple III, 2, 79, 102
Applesoft program, 74
Application, practical design, 81–99
Argument, 179
Arithmetic functions, 105–7
ASCII, 179
ASCII format, 77
@ASIN, 143–44
Assets, 82
@; see various functions
@ATAN, 144
Atari 800, 2
Attributes, 111–15
  submenu, 114
  uses, 111
/AV values, 114
@AVERAGE, 107, 145

B

Backup, 179
Backup procedures, 14–15
Balance sheet, 82–83
Basic accounting equation, 82–83
Basis codes, 88

Bents, Jerrold H., 63
Bistate conditions, 50
BYTE magazine, 38
Blank a cell, 46, 127, 179
Blank initialized disk, 34
Blank template, 84
Boole, George, 50
Boolean, 179
Boolean algebra, 50
Boolean functions, 50–55, 102
Borders, 29–30
BOT, beginning of template, 40
Bricklin, Daniel S., 2
Bug, 179

C

CalcPad, 16, 24
  coding sheet, 74
  planning sheet, 16
Calculation, 49–50
Calculation area
  intermediate, 17, 21
  template, 17–19
Carriage return, 179
Cell location symbol, 33
Cell references, 20–24
Cells, 179
  blanking out, 46
  protect and unprotect, 112–13
  source range, 6–8, 26–29
  target range, 6–8, 26–29
  VisiCalc, 5–6
Centronics printers, 36
@CHOOSE, 88, 106–7, 146
Circular references, 49–50, 180
Clearing memory, 118, 128
COGS ratio, 87

Column, 180
Columns
  global/nonglobal size, 120
  variable widths, 120
  widths, 26
Commands, 128–39, 180
  DIF, 136
  global, 24–26, 130–31
  print, 31–32, 132–33
  replicate, 6–8, 134–35
  rounding, 46–48
  saving and loading, 32
  storage, 134–36
  VisEXEC, 46
Compounding, 6, 92
Compressed type, 36–37
Computers; *see also* Microprocessor, *specific brands*
  bistate conditions of memory, 50
  memory location, 50
Consolidating, 75–77
  with Data Interchange Format, 61–63
Context Management System, 78
Control key, 180
Coordinate, 180
@COS, 147
@COUNT, 107, 147–48
Cursor, 180
Cursor cell, 180

D

Data, 180
Data area, 17–19
Data-base management programs, 75
Data Interchange Format (DIF), 32, 38–41, 59–63, 66, 75, 76, 78, 102
  column/row save command, 40–41
  consolidating with, 61–63
  RETURN command, 40–41
  rolling with, 60–61
  saving a file, 38–39
  SATN, No. 18, 38
  tuples and vectors, 39
  use, 59–63
Data sharing, 74–75
Date arithmetic functions, 107–9
@DAY, 107–9
Debug, 74, 180
Default attribute, 115
Default mode, 113
Defining ranges, 48–49
Designer, template, 4
DIF, 180; *see also* Data Interchange Format
Disks, 180
  backup, 14–15
  blank initialized, 34
  printing to, 37–38
Disk files, naming, 35
Disk full error, 34
Display format options, 24–26

Displaying values, 114–15
DocuCalc, 74, 84
DOS (Disk Operating System), 15–16
@DOTPROD, 105–6
Dow Jones News Retrieval Service (DJNS), 74–75

E

Electronic worksheet, 5
Ending inventory, 96
ELSE, 53
ENTER key, 25
@ERROR, 148
ESCAPE code, 37
Exec capability, 63
@EXP, 148–49
Expansion boards, 79
Exponent, 23, 92
Expression, 180
Expression attribute, 112

F

@FALSE, 51, 149
Farin, Thomas A., 63
Files, 180
  consolidating, 75–76
  Data Interchange Format, 38–42
  loading, 35–36
  naming, 35
  reading, 32–35
  saving and loading, 32–36
  sorting, 76
  storing, 14
  VisEXEC, 62–73
Financial functions, 103–5
Financial ratios, 89
Financial statements, 82–83
Floppy disk, 180
Format, 180
Format, global, 24–26, 85
Formatted disk, 34
Formulas, 5–6
Forward references, 49–50, 97, 181
Frankston, Robert, 2
Functions, 8–9, 181; *see also specific functions*
  arithmetic, 105–6
  date arithmetic, 107–9
  keys, 4
  page-print formatting, 122–23
  @SUM, 9
  VisiCalc financial, 103–5
@FV, 103–4

G

/GC command, 24–25
/GF command, 24
/GFG command, 24
Global commands, 24, 85, 181
Global default attribute, 115

Index

Global expression attribute, 112
Global format, 24–26
    column widths, 25
    manual recalculation, 25
    order of recalculation, 25–26
Global parameters, 33
/GO command, 24
/GOC command, 26
/GOR command, 26
/GR command, 24
/GRA command, 25
Graphing programs, 78
/GRM command, 25
Gutters, 114

H

Hard disk, 181
Hardware
    expansion boards, 79
    numeric key pad, 79
    output boards, 79
    VisiCalc enhancements, 79–80
Help screens, 118–20
Hewlett Packard computer, 2, 78
Hexadecimal, 181
Hide attribute, 112
@HMS, 107–9
Horizontal windowing, 20
@HOURS, 107–9

I

IBM Personal Computer, 2, 24, 77–78, 79, 102
@IF, 48, 87, 149
Income accounts, 83
Income taxes, 94–96
Individual Retirement Account (IRA), 22–23
Information, 5–6
Initialized diskette, 34
Input, 181
Insurance, 14
Interface card, 36–37
Intermediate calculation area, 21, 84, 95
@INT, 88
Internal rate of return, 104–5, 181
@IRR, 104–5
@ISERROR, 150–51
@ISNA, 151

K–L

Kalish, Candace E., 38
Keyboard enhancer, 80
Keypad, 79
Keystroke memory, 117–18
@LABEL, 106–7
Labels, 5–6, 181
    mode, 113
    with *gutters*, 114
    returning, 106–7
@LCHOOSE, 106–7

Liability, 82
Linefeed, 181
List, 181
@LN, 151
Load, 181
Loading files, 32, 36
Local formats, 29, 181
@LOG10, 152
Lookup code, 85
@LOOKUP, 106–7, 152
Lookup table, 87
Lotus Development Corporation, 78

M

MagicCalc, 2
Manual recalculations, 25
Mataya, L. Darryl, 63
@MAX, 107, 154
Mayer, Malinda F., 38
@MDY, 107–9
Memory
    allocation, 17
    erasing, 14
    management, 33
Microprocessors
    brands, 2
    losing memory, 14
    memory limitations, 5
@MIN, 107, 154–55
@MINUTES, 107–9
@MOD, 105–6
Mode attributes, 112–13
Modem, 77
@MONTH, 107–9
Multiple deletions, 121
Multiple insertions, 122
Multiple replications, 120–21
@MDY, 107–9

N

@NA, 103–4
Naming disk files, 35
Net present value, 156, 181
Nonexclusive OR, 52
@NOT, 155–56
@NPV, 156
Numbers, 5–6
    mode, 113
    rounding, 46–47
Numeric keypad, 79

O

Operating expenses, 83
Operating ratios, 89
@OR, 52, 156–57
Orderot recalculation, 25–26, 182
Output, 182
Output boards, 79
Overlays, 56–59, 182
Owners' equity, 82

P

/P command, 31–32, 36–38
Page-print formatting, 122–23
@PERIODS, 103–4
Peripherals, 73–80
@PI, 157
Planning, 16, 74
@PMT, 103–4
Preboot programs, 79
Printers, 36–37
   settings, 122–23
Printing, 36–38
   to disk, 37–38
   setup strings, 36–37
Projection, 182
Protect and unprotect attribute, 112–13
@PV, 103–4

Q–R

Quasi Boolean functions, 55
Radio Shack Model III, 77
RAM, 182
RAM expansion boards, 79
Ranges,
   defining, 48–49
   specifying, 9
   source/target, 6–8
@RATE, 103–4
Recalculation
   manual, 25
   order of, 25–26
Recursive, 182
Reformatting print to disk files, 75
REPLICATE command, 6–8
Replication, 6–8
   advanced version, 120–22
   formats, 29
   keystrokes, 28
   multiple, 120–21
   source/target ranges, 26–29
Report, 182
Report area, 17–19
Return key, 25
Roll, 182
   with DIF, 60–61
   with VisEXEC, 64–66
ROM, 182
@ROUND, 105
Rounding, 46–47
Row, 182

S

Saturn Systems, Inc., 79
Save, 182
Saving, 14, 32–36, 46; *see also* Storage
   parts of a template, 46
/S# command, 32
/S#L command, 32
/S#S command, 32
/SAVE command, 32

@SECONDS, 107–9
Setup, 36
Setup strings, 36–37
Sharing data, 74–75
Sinclair ZX-81 computer, 2
Single-entry variables, 21
/SL command, 32
Software, 183
   consolidating programs, 75–77
   data sharing, 74–75
   enhancements for VisiCalc, 73–79
   graphing programs, 78
   keyboard enhancer, 80
   modem, 77
   planning and debugging, 74
   talking to other computers, 77
   VersaCalc 16!, 73–74
   word processor interfaces, 78
Software Arts, Inc., 20, 38, 41, 63, 79
   Technical Note (SATN) No. 18, 38
Sorting, 76
Source range, 183
   of cells, 6–8
   replication, 26–29
Spreadsheet program, 2, 78
@SQRT, 158
/SS command, 32
Standard text files, 14–15
Statement
   cash flow, 83
   financial, 82–83
   income, 83
Storage
   back-up disks, 14–15
   back-up program, 15
   importance, 14
   standard text files, 14–15
@SUM, 9, 94, 158–59
SuperCalc, 2
Symbolic logic, 50

T

Tab attribute, 113–14
@TAN, 159
Target range, 183
   cells, 6–8
   replication, 26–29
Templates, 3, 183
   advanced design, 45–72
   back-up disks, 14–15
   blank, 30
   Boolean functions, 50–55
   calculation area, 17–19
   cell references, 20–24
   data area, 17–19
   defining ranges, 48–49
   design and use, 4
   designer, 4
   entering, 19–24
   forward references, 49–50

Index

Templates—*Cont.*
  global parameters, 24
  local formats, 29
  planning, 16–19
  practical application design, 84–99
  printing, 36–38
  replication, 26–29
  report area, 17–19
  saving and loading, 33–36
  saving parts of, 46
  storing, 14
  use of DIF, 59–63
  vertical/horizontal windowing, 20
  VisEXEC files, 63–72
  windows, 45–46
  worksheet overlays, 56–59
Textfile, 183
Timex 1000 computer, 2
Triangular references, 50
TRS-80 computers, 2; *see also* Radio Shack Model III
  memory expansion, 79
  Model I, 15–16
@TRUE, 51, 160
True-false Boolean values, 50–54
Tuples, 39

U–V

UPDATE file, 65
User, template, 4
User friendly templates, 113
User input, 84
VALUE function, 106–7
Values, 183
  attribute, 114–15
  displaying, 114–15
  mode, 113
Variable, 183
Variable column widths, 75–76, 79, 120
Variables, single-entry, 21, 93
VCAV; *see* VisiCalc Advanced Version
Vectors, 39, 183
VersaCalc 16!
  program, 63, 72
  uses, 73–74
Version, 15, 61, 102
Vertical windowing, 20
Videx Keyboard Enhancer, 80
VisEXEC, 183
  accumulating, 67–72
  commands, 46
  files, 63–72
  rolling with, 64–66
VisiCalc
  Apple computers, 15–16
  back-up program 15
  basic template design, 13–30
  built-in functions, 8–9
  cell numbering, 5
  Data Interchange Format, 38–42

VisiCalc—*Cont.*
  definition, 5
  display format options, 24–26
  enhanced features, 79
  entering a template, 19–24
  global commands, 24
  hardware enhancements, 79–80
  IBM Personal Computer, 15–16
  imitations of, 2
  importance a saving files, 14
  planning a template, 16–19
  practical application design, 81–99
  preboot programs, 79
  replication, 6–8
  rounding, 46–48
  screen, 7
  software enhancements, 73–79
  stages, 102
  types of information entered, 5–6
VisiCalc Advanced Version (VCAV), 102
  arithmetic functions, 105–7
  attributes, 111–15
  clearing memory, 118
  date arithmetic, 107–9
  features, 103–9
  financial functions, 103–5
  help screens, 118–20
  keystroke memory, 117–18
  lookup functions, 106–7
  multiple deletions, 121
  multiple insertions, 122
  multiple replications, 120–21
  page-print formatting, 122–23
  returning labels, 106–7
  variable column widths, 120
VisiCorp, 2, 15, 20, 77, 79, 102
VisiPlot, 38, 78
VisiTrend, 38, 78
@VMDV, 107–9
Volume Table of Contents (VTOC), 15n

W–Y

/W command, 20
/WH command, 20, 45
Windowing
  function, 45
  vertical and horizontal, 20
Windows, 20, 45
Word processor, 183
Word processor interfaces, 35, 78
Worksheet, 183
  accountant's, 5–6
  data/calculation/report areas, 17–19
  overlays, 56–59
  planning and debugging, 29
  saving, 46
  template planning, 16–17
/WV command, 20, 45
@YEAR, 107–9